IN THE SAME SERIES

The Return of the Reader

Reader-response criticism

ELIZABETH FREUND

METHUEN
London and New York

First published in 1987 by
Methuen & Co. Ltd
11 New Fetter Lane, London EC4P 4EE
Published in the USA by
Methuen & Co.
in association with Methuen, Inc.
29 West 35th Street, New York NY 10001

© 1987 Elizabeth Freund

Set by Hope Services, Abingdon
Printed in Great Britain
by Richard Clay (The Chaucer Press) Ltd
Bungay, Suffolk

British Library Cataloguing in
Publication Data

Freund, Elizabeth
The return of the reader: reader-response
criticism. – (New accents)
1. Reading, Psychology of
I. Title   II. Series
428.4'01'9   BF456.R2

ISBN 0 416 34400 3
      0 416 34410 0 Pbk

Library of Congress Cataloging in
Publication Data

Freund, Elizabeth.
The return of the reader.
(New accents)
Bibliography: p.
Includes index.
1. Reader-response criticism.   I. Title.
II. Series: New accents (Methuen & Co.)
PN98.R38F7 1987   801'.95   86–33295

ISBN 0 416 34400 3
      0 416 34410 0 (pbk.)

To my mother
and to the memory of my father

Contents

General editor's preface

It is easy to see that we are living in a time of rapid and radical social change. It is much less easy to grasp the fact that such change will inevitably affect the nature of those disciplines that both reflect our society and help to shape it.

Yet this is nowhere more apparent than in the central field of what may, in general terms, be called literary studies. Here, among large numbers of students at all levels of education, the erosion of the assumptions and presuppositions that support the literary disciplines in their conventional form has proved fundamental. Modes and categories inherited from the past no longer seem to fit the reality experienced by a new generation.

New Accents is intended as a positive response to the initiative offered by such a situation. Each volume in the series will seek to encourage rather than resist the process of change; to stretch rather than reinforce the boundaries that currently define literature and its academic study.

Some important areas of interest immediately present themselves. In various parts of the world, new methods of analysis have been developed whose conclusions reveal the limitations of the Anglo-American outlook we inherit. New concepts of literary forms and modes have been proposed; new notions of the nature of literature itself and of how it communicates are current; new views of literature's role in relation to society flourish. *New Accents* will aim to expound and comment upon the most notable of these.

In the broad field of the study of human communication, more and more emphasis has been placed upon the nature and function of the new electronic media. *New Accents* will try to identify and discuss the challenge these offer to our traditional modes of critical response.

The same interest in communication suggests that the series should also concern itself with those wider anthropological and sociological areas of investigation which have begun to involve scrutiny of the nature of art itself and of its relation to our whole way of life. And this will ultimately require attention to be focused on some of those activities which in our society have hitherto been excluded from the prestigious realms of Culture. The disturbing realignment of values involved and the disconcerting nature of the pressures that work to bring it about both constitute areas that *New Accents* will seek to explore.

Finally, as its title suggests, one aspect of *New Accents* will be firmly located in contemporary approaches to language, and a continuing concern of the series will be to examine the extent to which relevant branches of linguistic studies can illuminate specific literary areas. The volumes with this particular interest will nevertheless presume no prior technical knowledge on the part of their readers, and will aim to rehearse the linguistics appropriate to the matter in hand, rather than to embark on general theoretical matters.

Each volume in the series will attempt an objective exposition of significant developments in its field up to the present as well as an account of its author's own views of the matter. Each will culminate in an informative bibliography as a guide to further study. And, while each will be primarily concerned with matters relevant to its own specific interests, we can hope that a kind of conversation will be heard to develop between them; one whose accents may perhaps suggest the distinctive discourse of the future.

TERENCE HAWKES

Acknowledgements

I should like to acknowledge the help I have received at various stages from many friends and colleagues. The valuable comments and conversation of Shlomith Rimmon-Kenan, Rael Meyerowitz, Josh Wilner, Michael Goldman and Wolfgang Iser have contributed to the shape of this book. The pervasive influence of Geoffrey Hartman over a number of years has been beyond anxiety.

I am particularly grateful to John Landau who read and reread generously and untiringly and to Baruch Hochman whose timely alarm prompted me to rethink my expository intentions. Above all I wish to thank Ruth Nevo whose 'brightening glance', intellectual enthusiasm and editorial skills have been the *sine qua non* of all my work. My thanks also go to the many students who have accompanied my readings in literary theory in recent years, and to Eugene Sotirescu for technical assistance.

I should also like to express my gratitude to Terence Hawkes for his encouragement and scrupulous reading of the manuscript, and to Janice Price for her kindness and patience, as well as to the editors at Methuen for help in preparing the manuscript for publication.

My son Gil forebore my spasmodic writing habits with remarkable tolerance and good humour – thank you, Gil. My deepest debt of gratitude is expressed in my dedication.

The House Was Quiet and the World Was Calm

The house was quiet and the world was calm.
The reader became the book; and summer night

Was like the conscious being of the book.
The house was quiet and the world was calm.

The words were spoken as if there was no book,
Except that the reader leaned above the page,

Wanted to lean, wanted much most to be
The scholar to whom his book is true, to whom

The summer night is like a perfection of thought.
The house was quiet because it had to be.

The quiet was part of the meaning, part of the mind:
The access of perfection to the page.

And the world was calm. The truth in a calm world,
In which there is no other meaning, itself

Is calm, itself is summer and night, itself
Is the reader leaning late and reading there.

Wallace Stevens

Introduction:
the order of reading

In his well-known study of Romanticism, M.H. Abrams draws
the following diagram to depict four basic terms in 'the total
situation' of the work of art (*The Mirror and the Lamp*, p. 6):

This triangle represents the basic co-ordinates of critical
orientation in satellite formation. At the centre is the work or
artefact itself. In orbit around it, at equidistant points, are the
other three basic elements that constitute the object of critical
investigation. These are the work's producer, the state of
affairs ('nature' or the universe of existing things) which the
work reflects or signifies, and the audience to which it is
addressed. A comprehensive critical approach, Abrams points
out, will strive to give an account of all four terms and the
relations between them. But the history of criticism reveals
that at different times this or that element has been privileged,
temporarily eclipsing the importance of the others. Thus, a
focus on the work itself, Abrams says, will yield a so-called
objective approach, on the artist an *expressive* approach, on the
universe a *mimetic* approach, and on the audience a *pragmatic*

approach. Each shift of emphasis from one term to the other will yield a different critical orientation.

What Abrams does not say, however (evidently because he does not believe it to be the case), is that such a shift in emphasis can effectively undermine the fixed centre of his triangle and with it the entire ideological slant which ascribes a privileged and fixed position to the work of art at the centre of this constellation. The emblem of the triangle at once advertises an underlying (perhaps unconscious) prejudice and also conceals it by the seemingly innocent analogy of a neutral unilateral geometry. In other words, Abrams's implicit presupposition is that these terms are fixed and determinate points of reference in a universal and timeless 'total situation', and that different aspects of the critical sky will come into view depending on the gazer's angle of vision and/or his/her historical context. But this latter qualification – the enfranchisement of the viewer's perspective – is precisely the feature which introduces the subversive possibility that each term in the 'total situation' is radically unstable or indeterminate, a product of the beholder's gaze. Some such eventuality is indeed the outcome – or, at any rate, the thrust – of the recent shift of interest to the bottom right-hand corner of Abrams's triangle. The drift of the 'pragmatic' or, as it is nowadays called, reader-response orientation in critical theory challenges the privileged position of the work of art and seeks to undermine its priority and authority not only by displacing the work from the centre and substituting the reader in its place, but by putting in doubt the autonomy of the work and, in certain cases, even causing the work to 'vanish' altogether. This turn of events is the subject of this introductory book.

The turn to the reader

> It is difficult to read. The page is dark.
> Yet he knows what it is that he expects.
> (Wallace Stevens, 'Phosphor Reading by His Own Light')

The view that a text cannot live in isolation from a context of reading and response has acquired the force of a cliché mainly because the text's natural companion, the reader, slips so easily into the category of that which goes without saying. The inherent privacy and silence of reading have no doubt encouraged a tendency to suppress the embarrassment of subjectivity, placing it beyond the pale of a critical decorum which aspires to be objective. 'However disciplined by taste and skill', says Northrop Frye in his *Anatomy of Criticism* (1957), 'the experience of literature is, like literature itself, unable to speak.' So-called affective theory, W.K. Wimsatt argued, has often proved less a scientific view of literature than an empty prerogative to report experiences such as 'tears, prickles or other physiological symptoms'. The less said about these vague 'states of emotional disturbance' the better for our critical manners and for the promotion of a truly objective criticism.

> The more specific the account of the emotion induced by a poem, the more nearly it will be an account of the reasons for emotion, the poem itself, and the more reliable it will be as an account of what the poem is likely to induce in other – sufficiently informed – readers. It will in fact supply the kind of information which will enable readers to respond to the poem.
>
> (1970a, p. 34, first published 1954)

Whether the logic of these two sentences suffers from a genetic fallacy or a tautology is not so pertinent here as the fact that the sense contrives ambivalently to include and exclude the reader in one movement, entangling subject and object (or the emotion and the reason for the emotion) so irreducibly as to convey a double and contradictory message, one half of which must be suppressed in the interests of coherence. The move deserves notice because it betrays the characteristically uneasy relationship adopted by New Criticism to the question of the reader. By positing a continuity between the poem and the reader's response, Wimsatt concedes that some mode of reader-response criticism must be adduced; at the same time, reader response (and, by extension, the danger of its aberrant subjectivity, multiplicity, idiosyncrasy and so forth) is rendered extraneous by its identification with a single structure of emotion which is already inscribed in and governed by 'the poem itself'. (Indeed, there is even some doubt whether 'reading', as opposed to 'criticism', produces anything more than neurological reactions. We can note the rhetorical manoeuvre which dissociates readers from critics by the insinuation that without the latter's assistance, the former are altogether unable to respond!)

Underlying Wimsatt's prescription is a traditional, rigidly hierarchical, view of the text–reader relationship. The poem itself, enshrined as the prime mover of all meanings and emotions, governs the hierarchy. Subject to its dominion is the disinterested critic who performs the task of giving an 'account' by approximating the meaning and mediating the textual properties. Last comes the lowly reader who benefits passively from the critic's work. Since response, in this benevolently despotic arrangement, is not a property of the reader at all but something inscribed in and controlled by 'the poem itself', the reader need only be taken for granted. Taken for granted, readers and reading become invisible, mute, imperceptible, ghostly.

If New Criticism frowned upon categories of analysis 'extraneous' to the object, it positively bristled with contempt for anything so brazen as a personality in the critic. 'The critic . . . if he is to justify his existence, should endeavour to discipline his personal prejudices and cranks – tares to which we are all subject – and compose his differences with as many of his fellows as possible, in the common pursuit of true judgment': thus Eliot in 'The function of criticism' (1932, p. 25, first published 1923), an essay in which he shrilly endeavours to compose his differences with Middleton Murry by lambasting Murry's presumptuous licensing of the protestant vulgarity of an 'inner voice'. ('The possessors of the inner voice', declares the high priest of impersonality, 'ride ten in a compartment to a football match at Swansea, listening to the inner voice, which breathes the eternal message of vanity, fear, and lust' (p. 27).) Cooler but no less firm was Wimsatt's repudiation of the carnal nature of 'affective' criticism. 'The report of some reader . . . that a poem or story induces in them vivid images, intense feelings, or heightened consciousness, is neither anything which can be refuted nor anything which it is possible for the objective critic to take into account. The purely affective report is either too physiological or it is too vague' (1970a, p. 32, first published 1954).

The demand that criticism be cognitive, not emotive, has also contributed in no small degree to the consolidation of stylistic norms for the writing of critical prose. The rule of impersonality (whose effects manifest themselves so frequently in our professional journals) has cultivated an insipid style of chaste and aseptic neutrality which pretends that the critic is as free of quirks and oddities, and of linguistic mischief, as he is of ideological and psychological motives.[1]

However, the conspiracy of silence surrounding the supposed impersonality of critical reading and writing is now gradually being unmasked. The 'turn' loosely called 'reader-response criticism' attempts to make the imperceptible process of reading perceptible by seeking to reopen to scrutiny that which has been declared inscrutable, illegitimate or trivial. It braves the ghost with a challenge to stand and unfold itself. In the last fifteen years or so, an intense concern with the text–reader relationship, with the reading process, with our acts of understanding and interpretation, and with the subject of the 'subject' has been occupying the forefront of Anglo-American critical attention. Broadly speaking, this constitutes a movement away from the positivistic assumptions of formalism and New Criticism with respect to the objectivity and self-sufficiency of the literary text. In one mode or another, the swerve to the reader assumes that our relationship to reality is not a positive knowledge but a hermeneutic construct, that all perception is already an act of interpretation, that the notion of a 'text-in-itself' is empty, that a poem cannot be understood in isolation from its results, and that subject and object are indivisibly bound. By refocusing attention on the reader, reader-response criticism attempts to grapple with questions generally ignored by schools of criticism which teach us how to read; questions such as *why* do we read and what are the deepest sources of our engagement with literature? what does reading have to do with the life of the psyche, or the imagination, or our linguistic habits? what happens – consciously or unconsciously, cognitively or psychologically – during the reading process? Reader-response criticism probes the practical or theoretical consequences of the event of reading by further asking what the relationship is between the private and the public, or how and where meaning is made, authenticated and authorized, or why readers agree or disagree about their interpretations. In doing so it ventures to reconceptualize the terms of the text–reader interaction. A by-product of these investigations is a renewed attention to the different aspects and implications – rhetorical, political, cultural, psychological, etc. – of critical style. The label 'reader-response criticism', loosely taken, designates this heterogeneous field of interests. In its variegated forms, reader-response criticism undertakes to narrativize, characterize and personify or otherwise objectify the reading experience and its conditions. It undertakes, in short, to make the implicit features of 'reading' explicit.

The subject/object of inquiry

> For Literature is like phosphorus: it shines with its maximum brilliance at the moment when it attempts to die.
> (Roland Barthes, *Writing Degree Zero*)

The field at first glance seems to partake of the tumult of Babel. To characterize reader-response criticism as a new order or a monolith of any sort would be a flagrant distortion of the plurality of voices and approaches, of the theoretical and methodological heterogeneity, and of the ideological divergences which shelter under the umbrella of this appellation. The trend to liberate the reader from his enforced anonymity and silence, to enable him to recover an identity or the authority of a voice, is bedevilled by all the concomitant hazards, schisms, anxieties and jargons of liberation movements. Indeed the first thing to be safely said about the subject is that it is a labyrinth of converging and sometimes contradictory approaches. In Susan Suleiman's apt figure, reader-response criticism follows 'not a single widely trodden path but a multiplicity of criss-crossing, often divergent tracks that cover a vast area of the critical landscape whose complexity dismays the brave and confounds the faint of heart' (Suleiman and Crosman 1980, p. 6).

Certainly, the traveller in these regions encounters a disorderly scene crowded with explorers whose discrepant maps rechart the topography along the changing landmarks of phenomenology, structuralism, semiotics, rhetoric, psycho-analysis, transactive criticism, subjective criticism, feminism, psychoaesthetics, deconstruction, gnostic revisionism, and other critical and philosophical persuasions. Agreement about the lie of the land is rare, for each explorer within this heteronomous company seems to be either armed with a different map or reading the same map differently. Nor is there any accord regarding the identity of the subject under investigation. The concept 'audience' or 'reader' may be anything from an idealized construct to an actual historical idiosyncratic personage, including the author. Personifications – the mock reader (Gibson), the implied reader (Booth, Iser), the model reader (Eco), the super-reader (Riffaterre), the inscribed or encoded reader (Brooke-Rose), the narratee (Prince), the ideal reader (Culler), the literent (Holland), the actual reader (Jauss), the informed reader or the interpretive community (Fish) – proliferate. Aside from the loosely shared belief that a poem cannot mean or in some cases even exist in dissociation from its effects, the theoretical grounds or presuppositions underlying reader-response criticism will vary from one case to the next.

The vast spectrum of theoretical and ideological positions is due in no small measure to the fact that in a post-Freudian, post-Marxist, post-Saussurean age, the Anglo-American literary critic has become increasingly aware of the non-insularity of his discipline, situated as it is within a vital network of relationships which constitute the pluralistic cultural ambience the human sciences inhabit today. The bewildering multipli-cation of textual and discursive milieus has given rise to a new need to question, review and make explicit the methodological and theoretical assumptions and intentions underlying critical practice. This self-conscious moment has brought about a vigorous reassessment of our primary concepts: the notion of 'text' or 'work of art', the notion of 'author', the meaning of 'meaning', its locus, determination and the sources of its authority, the 'rhetoricity' of language, the conditions of intelligibility which govern reading and the vagaries of interpretation. Argument over these issues is often conducted in an embattled style, a rhetoric of 'crisis', which pronounces the deaths of authors, subjects and liberal humanism, or celebrates the values of an energizing pluralism. It speaks of 'impasses' and 'aporias', of 'negative' hermeneutics and 'criticism in the wilderness' but is also passionately and scrupulously concerned with the refining and redefining of its positions and values, and with 'saving' the text and the 'subject'. A glance at any one of our professional journals will instantly reveal that the move to re-examine or revise the implications of the text–reader relationship can range anywhere between confident accounts, on the one hand, of the inflexible constraints which control, inform and validate the reading process, and vigorously polemical explorations, on the other, of the text's indeterminacy, opacity and unreadability. A typical instance of the nature and tone of the controversy can be found in the proceedings of the 1976 Convention of the Modern Language Association: its Forum on 'The limits of pluralism' (to which Wayne C. Booth, M.H. Abrams and J. Hillis Miller contributed talks subsequently published in *Critical Inquiry*, 3 (1977)), has become a kind of handy signpost pointing to the bewildering but also exhilarating juncture of self-scrutiny and heated debate at which students, teachers and makers of literary theory find themselves today.

In the light of this turbulent disarray, and perceived within the general trend towards self-reflexiveness in literary discourse, reader-response theories are like what Wittgenstein described as a family the members of which do not all possess the same common physical characteristics but nevertheless display likenesses to each other. Thus, the categories of reader-response criticism frequently overlap, but distinctions between them may blur, focus or collapse depending on the angle of vision, point of departure or context of inquiry. The formidable task of providing a preliminary guide for the perplexed has been effectively tackled by the excellent editorial introductions to two volumes of essays on the subject, to both of which I am deeply indebted. In her remarkably informative, even-handed and wide-ranging introduction to a volume of commissioned essays on *The Reader in the Text: Essays on Audience and Interpretation* (1980), Susan R. Suleiman outlines six contemporary varieties or approaches: rhetorical, semiotic and structuralist, phenomenological, subjective and psychological, historical and sociological, and hermeneutic, all of which serve as a grid or frame of reference on which particular instances of reader-oriented criticisms (which often have recourse to more than one approach) may be charted. Jane P. Tompkins, in her anthology entitled *Reader-Reponse Criticism: From Formalism to Post-Structuralism* (1980), gathers together a selection of previously published essays by several hands. The conjunction and sequence of pieces[2] enables her to outline a narrative of the evolving erosion and ultimate destruction of the objective status of the text, and to show that '[w]hat began as a small shift of emphasis ends by becoming an exchange of world views' (p. x).

My own purpose is to offer detailed critical reviews of the work of several reader-response critics[3] who represent some of the major trends in what strikes me as a distinctly Anglo-American institutional phenomenon, starting with the pioneering explorations of I.A. Richards in the aesthetics of response, and concluding with some of the current post-structuralist American speculations on the problematics of 'reading'. It is not accidental that critical narratives come into being as family romances. Critics no less than other writers create their own precursors, as Borges might say, by a process of evading, selecting or rejecting imaginary or real models of priority or authority in the interests of fashioning a fable of identity. These acts of 'misprision', to borrow Harold Bloom's concept, considerably complicate any historical–genealogical account of the development of a critical movement, and it is with this proviso in mind that I make the claim that the impulse to a theorization of reading came into being not only with the early work of Richards but also, albeit indirectly, with the New Criticism. The central part of my survey addresses itself to the endeavours of four critics – Jonathan Culler, Stanley Fish, Norman Holland and Wolfgang Iser – whose respective programmes for a reader-oriented criticism arise from the perspectives of French structuralism, American rhetorical and stylistic criticism, Freudian psychoanalysis and the German school of *Rezeptionsästhetik*.

I shall anticipate my account of the reversals and discoveries informing the progress of affective poetics by remarking that, despite the differences in premises and philosophical orientation,

I discern a common pattern of development, a recurrent plot, shared by these projects. Crudely summarized, the point of departure in each story is always a dissatisfaction with formalist principles, and a recognition that the practice of supposedly impersonal and disinterested reading is never innocent and always infected by suppressed or unexamined presuppositions. The dramatic action begins with a challenge to the doctrine of the text's priority and self-sufficiency. In its first phase the conflict is conducted, roughly speaking, by reversing the (implicit or explicit) hierarchy of the text–reader pair. By refocusing attention on the reader instead of the text as the source of literary meaning, a new field of inquiry is opened up. But when this exchange is discovered to perpetuate rather than escape a determinate and positivistic structure of hierarchies, a further sequence of displacements and substitutions is introduced to erode the distance between the redefined terms until the irksome dichotomy of reader/text is abolished by an assimilation of the text into the reader or the reader into the text. The outcome of this turn of events is to undermine the reader-response project, for when the discrete concepts of 'reader' and 'text' lose their specific difference the *raison d'etre* for both a *text*-centred and a *reader*- or *self*-centred criticism is undone; 'reading and writing . . . become distinguishable only as two names for the same activity' (Tompkins 1980, p. x), a praxis to which the post-structuralist name of 'textuality' is frequently given. In this last phase of 'reading-as-textuality', reader-response criticism as a coherent, total and theoretically viable project is extinguished, though not before some previously darkened or neglected feature of the text–reader relationship has been illuminated in the momentary flare. (The case of Stanley Fish's affective poetics is prototypical.) Indeed, one of the more intriguing aspects of the short theoretical life-spans of these projects is the discovery of their own self-consuming, self-transcending, or self-deconstructing energies.

This book, then, is not a prolegomenon to the possibility of a future lectocentric criticism, because one of its conclusions is that reader-response criticism, on the evidence of its own premises, suggests that it has a past rather than a future. Nor do I offer new or alternative theoretical grounds for critical practice – the reader will select or creatively synthesize his own – since my main contention, if any, is that a perusal of critical theory leads to an enhanced awareness of the limits of its usefulness, and of the perishability of its prescriptive authority. Roland Barthes's stricture, that a methodology 'that unceasingly declares its will-to-methodology always becomes sterile in the end', is repeatedly vindicated by the narratives I am about to unfold. 'At some point one has to turn against the method, or at least to treat it without any founding privilege' (quoted by Harari 1979, p. 10). It is an awareness of the insufficiency of theoretical and methodological borders, the infinitizing or receding movement of their horizons or, better yet, the moment of recoil from any totalizing act of the mind, that I hope to accentuate in my discussions.

Theory of reading

> To see this age! A sentence is but a chev'ril glove to a good wit. How quickly the wrong side may be turned outward!
> (Shakespeare, *Twelfth Night*, III.i)

It is the vexed question of the locus, validity and authority of textual meaning that gives rise to the game of musical chairs intimated by Abrams's map. In more recent publications Abrams notes with alarm that under the aegis of Derrida and deconstruction[4] the new 'Age of Reading' has played havoc with our received notions of the circuit of communication, and of authorial and textual authority. Parisian fashions, he feels, have 'dehumanized' the subject (be he/she author or reader) by replacing him/her with the notion of the text as 'a sealed echo-chamber in which meanings are reduced to a ceaseless echolalia, a vertical and lateral reverberation from sign to sign of ghostly nonpresence emanating from no voice, intended by no one, referring to nothing, bombinating in a void' (1977, p. 431). The charged rhetoric of this caricature is one instance of the polemical style in which the battle between the old-fashioned and the new-fangled is often conducted. Abrams is, of course, a defender of the 'traditional or humanistic paradigm of the writing and reading of literature', which is constructed on the following principles:

The writer is conceived, in Wordsworth's terms, as 'a man speaking to men'. Literature, in other words, is a transaction between a human author and his human reader. By his command of linguistic and literary possibilities, the author actualizes and records in words what he undertakes to signify of human beings and actions and about matters of human concern, addressing himself to those readers who are competent to understand what he has written. The reader sets himself to make out what the author has designed and signified, through putting into play a linguistic and literary expertise that he shares with the author. By approximating what the author undertook to signify the reader understands what the language of the work means.

(1979, p. 566)

In this model of reading, the literary text is a unique, complete and self-sufficient linguistic entity whose recognized presence or fullness is the object of critical exegesis: a form of communication strung between the poles of author and reader, who share codes ('linguistic and literary expertise') for the transmission and reception of a determinate core of meaning (see also 1977, p. 246). (Probably the best-known and most theoretically sophisticated model of this kind is Roman Jakobson's (1960).) The reader/critic's function, as in Wimsatt's premises, is to come as close as possible to the intention or literary message embedded in the text.

Informing this model is what Geoffrey Hartman has called a 'dream of communication' and intelligibility, one of whose effects has been the suppression or exclusion of alternative – 'impure', or less catholic, more intense and philosophically-inclined – styles or modes of understanding. The terms which underwrite the mainstream native tradition of critical activity, of which Abrams is a spokesman, are derived from and legislated by what Hartman calls the 'Arnoldian Concordat', a denomination for the tacit understanding 'which assigns to criticism a specific, delimited sphere distinct from the creative' (1980, p. 6), a secondary, servicing and serviceable function to be performed in the shadow of the primary text. The Age of Reading, or – as Hartman prefers to call it – 'philosophical' or 'revisionary' criticism, questions the metaphysical and epistemological presuppositions governing this arrangement and 'urges that readers, inspired by hermeneutic traditions, take back some of their authority, as in days of old' (p. 161). It is important to take note of the fact (of which Hartman repeatedly reminds us: see also 1983, 1984) that an alternative, albeit oft-forgotten or suppressed tradition of criticism, neither new-fangled nor modishly French but indigenous and 'Teufel-dröckhian' (p. 49), has been with us all along. The seemingly new-fangled critique of intelligibility does not spring fully-formed from the brain of any post-structuralist or 'uncanny' critic but has a native (largely romanticist) history of its own. This alternative mode of criticism may be yet another restless ghost, the dark shadow of whose otherness returns to haunt the institution.

What is at stake in the call to readers to take back some of their authority? When I speak of the *turn* to the reader or the *return* of the reader I invoke a resourceful pair of words denoting, among other things, circling and revolution; change of position, direction or quality; a trope or a translation; a replacement; a recurrence. Suleiman points out that, by and large, the turn to the reader has been a gradual and tranquil revolution: 'simply a shift in perspective, a new way of *seeing* what had always been there' (1980, p. 3, my emphasis). There is a paradox, familiar to interpreters, lurking here. To descry 'what had always been there' suggests that criticism, like reading itself, undertakes a complex detour to discover what it had always known. It inhabits a space which in hermeneutic theory is called a 'circle', a term used to describe how, 'in the process of understanding and interpretation, part and whole are related in a circular way: in order to understand the whole, it is necessary to understand the parts, while to understand the parts it is necessary to have some comprehension of the whole' (Hoy 1980, p. vii, first published 1978). Reading, we might then hypothesize, is a strenuous but perhaps not very purposeful mode of work; a species of revolving or shuttling – which may turn out to be a dangerously vertiginous movement. In another association, this (re)turn resembles what the psychoanalysts call the return of the repressed: the resurgence into visibility of a buried and unresolved conflict from the past, a knowledge one would have preferred to keep hidden or suppressed in the unconscious, a ghost come back to invade the present. One obvious implication of this intricate and multiplex analogy between the return of the repressed and the return of the reader is that reading is a species of self-discovery, but it may also be a neurosis or hysteria. (Reading has been compared to voyeurism by an eminent psychoanalyst.) The effects of such a (re)turn may be benignly therapeutic or profoundly troubling and disconcerting. Reading, as in the analytic situation, encompasses both text and interpreter, and may be seen as a species of transference, a mode of interaction in which the analyst's reading of the analysand has the uncanny effect of turning into the analysand's reading of the analyst. Either way, reading narrativizes, or tropes, or translates, or reorders, or places a new (b)order on what is inchoately 'there' and, in this sense, reading becomes a species of writing. But I am running ahead of myself by collapsing several intuitions and hypothetical narratives into a rather cryptic series of metaphors and allusions.

The fact is that the perceptual turn called reading, in order to enable the reader to find his tongue, to speak of (represent) her experience, does indeed engender a host of figures to name or impersonate a great variety of theoretical positions and presuppositions. Before I go any further, therefore, I should like to make a little more visible some of my own positions and presuppositions with respect to the reading of 'theory'.

Reading of theory

The library is unlimited and cyclical. If an eternal traveller were to cross it in any direction, after centuries he would see that the same volumes were repeated in the same disorder (which thus repeated would be an order: the Order). My solitude is gladdened by this elegant hope.

(Jorge Luis Borges, 'The Library of Babel')

The metaphor of viewing, one of several which I summon in the foregoing paragraphs, is not accidental, and in this connection it is useful to recall that the word 'theory' comes from the Greek root meaning 'a looking at', the same root that gives us the word 'theatre'. In this radical sense theory is what

I.A. Richards called 'a speculative instrument', a provisional point of view or a stance of spectatorship which provides a point of entry into a dramatic embroilment rather than establishing a stable ground outside it on which to construct a durable edifice of objective knowledge and observation. The abstract level of discourse we conventionally think of as 'theory' – a discourse which attempts to formulate, conceptualize and generalize the underlying principles of certain phenomena – does not occupy a privileged position beyond or above or outside the phenomena it probes. Theory remains a point of view, or a figuring forth, even when it attempts to describe the conditions of viewing.

What difference then does theory make? Obviously it is an essential aid to reflection and understanding, to what Hartman calls 'the life of the mind'. No criticism can take place without its ordering energy. In an essay entitled 'Unpacking my library', Walter Benjamin notes that 'if there is a counterpart to the confusion of a library it is the order of its catalogue' (1969, p. 60). Theory is that necessary (and arbitrary or proprietory) counterpart. For I.A. Richards, the seminal reader-response critic, 'order' (whose agency is rhetoric itself) was an indispensable concept to think with because 'all thinking from the lowest to the highest – whatever else it may be – is sorting' (1936, p. 30). And even the New Critics, so frequently and incorrectly maligned for their anti-theoretical bias, were perfectly aware of a reciprocity between the poles of a random and disorderly study of poems, and the regulating, ordering, systematizing force of theory.

> The good critic cannot stop with studying poetry, he must also study poetics. . . . Theory, which is expectation, always determines criticism, and never more than when it is unconscious. The reputed condition of no-theory in the critic's mind is illusory, and a dangerous thing in this occupation, which demands the utmost general intelligence, including perfect self-consciousness.
>
> (J.C. Ransom 1938, pp. 173–4)

If theory, as Ransom suggests, is an order of expectations, consider the concatenation of senses the notion of 'order' brings into play. (Etymologically, the word 'order' means a straight row or regular series, and it comes from the same Indo-European root which gives us the word 'art'.) Conscious or unconscious, theory is an independent 'order' in the sense that it is a regulating principle prior in rank and being to the study of particular works. This priority presupposes some definite plan or system, some condition in which everything is in its proper place; a system in which the class of poetics is set off from and governs the random disorder of the reading of individual texts. To invoke an order is not only to claim intelligibility; it is also to invoke some notion of a scale of being or a disposition of things in which the conditions of mastery and authority (or, alternatively, the solace and sanction of a brotherhood or community) are evident to all. The temptation to reify such an order into the reflection of a 'natural' state of affairs instead of viewing it as a culturally determined artifice, an institution, is what frequently animates the theoretical impulse.

All these things, and others, are presupposed by the order of theory. But does this mean that theory and practice coexist in serene reciprocity? And where is the order of (behind) the order? '[A]ny order', Benjamin says (1969, p. 60), 'is a balancing act of extreme precariousness'.

The assumptions I am outlining demarcate a persistent problem. The necessary theoretical and speculative props on which thought stands so precariously (by which, indeed, thought is constituted) should not be confused with firm ground. The belief that we read and interpret without any theoretical assumptions or prejudices is a delusion. If there is no immaculate perception, and intelligibility is bound by some determined (even if unconscious) system, then the life of the mind – if it is to maintain itself as such – will require that we probe and interrogate, make explicit, precisely by *reading* the circumference of the system underlying our reading practices. But the belief that we can govern particular readings and interpretations by an appeal to a general and universally valid or agreed-upon account of interpretation – an account which will stand beyond interpretation – may be equally deluded, for there appears to be no Archimedean fulcrum, no final metalinguistic resting place in which our probings and interrogations can lodge themselves. Every theory is language-bound, viz. another text to be read. You could say, aphoristically, that the doing and undoing of theory is theory's linguistic destiny. As in the Borgesian allegory ('The Library of Babel', 1962), our texts are an unending library whose circumference is inaccessible. The bibliophile's dream of a catalogue of catalogues (a general theory of the library) is just that – the expression of a wish or 'elegant hope'.

Perhaps that is why 'the attempt to establish an objective or scientific hermeneutics' begins to acquire the semblance of 'an act of defensive mastery. *It seeks to keep an unruly, changeable language within the bounds of intelligibility*' (Hartman 1976, p. 218, my emphasis). In a recent and controversial essay, Knapp and Michaels argue pragmatically that 'theory is nothing else but the attempt to escape practice' and, if that is the case, theory is a waste of time, or even an act of bad faith. Theory in their definition 'is the name for all the ways people have tried to stand outside practice in order to govern practice from without. Our thesis has been that no one can reach a position outside practice, that theorists should stop trying, and that the theoretical enterprise should therefore come to an end' (1982, p. 742).[5] In effect, this position rejects theory (and *a fortiori* the possibility of a benevolent reciprocity between theory and practice) because of its veiled politics, its unacknowledged will-to-power over the text. But to adopt this view is to be thrown back to the disorder and the blind self-delusion of 'no-theory'.

I am aware that these desperately abbreviated remarks cut across vast tracts of complex and paradoxical argumentation, to rehearse which is beyond the scope of this book. My basic point, however, is simple. Because concepts present themselves in linguistic form, 'theory' is made, and made available, in an exceedingly over-determined and unreliable medium. What is at stake is not only the intelligibility of theory but the intelligibility of language itself. On this issue, theory of reading runs into and collides with the reading of theory.

Reductively put, whether foundationalist or anti-foundationalist, theory exists as a text, a literary representation, and thus necessarily remains contaminated, indebted to rhetoricity and to the thousand natural shocks that representation is heir to. Theory finds itself embodied in the cognitive wiles of tropes and figures. It harbours the deposits of unconscious and disjunctive meanings, the ambiguities and uncertainties which we are normally content to attribute to literary language but shrink from in our expository discourse. Every student of a literary text is familiar to a greater or lesser extent with the promiscuous instability of literary meaning, and with the vagaries of interpretation this instability gives rise to. (This is not a deconstructionist discovery, although deconstruction as a strategy of reading has fostered and reinforced a vigilant and acutely self-conscious habit of textual scrutiny, with whose impetus I clearly sympathize.) Fundamental to twentieth-century critical thought is the understanding that, in a signifying system such as language, the signifier never coincides with the signified; one of these elements is always, so to speak, outstripping or in excess of the other. For practical purposes, what this means is that language is always in some degree unstable, indeterminate, double, duplicitous, other to itself, different – and therefore subject to misinterpretation. This seems to be the case whatever hermeneutic discipline we subscribe to, and whatever text (literary or theoretical) we read. And if that is the case, '[h]ow are literary studies ever to get started', Paul de Man asked (1972, p. 185), 'when every proposed method seems based on a misreading and a misconceived preconception about the nature of literary language?'

That they nevertheless get started and frequently thrive is beyond dispute. But in the absence of agreement about the nature of language, the speculative enterprise of literary theory and – with respect to our own concerns in this introductory review – the various attempts to establish a reader-response criticism, shrink or dissolve into the larger nexus of problems inhabiting the language in which such speculations are incarnated. Reading-oriented criticism is the smaller probe, as it were, within the larger nexus, which entails a reopening (perhaps an infinitizing) of the question of the authority or grounding force we desire to claim for the negotiation of our meanings or our knowledge.

Of the manifold consequences of this linguistic mischief, I shall here emphasize only the following. If theoretical or philosophical discourse has no privileged status, no purified metalanguage in which to conduct and express its investigations, it must be read in a double movement: on the one hand, with the same provisional trust or credence, and on the other with the same suspicious scrutiny, the same closeness of attention that is given literary language. The 'critical difference' today, as Barbara Johnson puts it, has to do with the fact that '[d]ifference . . . is at work within the very discourse of theory itself' (1980, p. xi). Since it is this 'difference' (theory's moment of recoil from itself) that I shall be frequently drawing attention to, I must ask my reader to bear in mind that the so-called 'crisis' of contemporary criticism (which repeatedly emphasizes the etymological relationship of 'crisis' to 'criticism') arises with the problem of understanding 'understanding', and that no discourse, even that of primers, is transparent or innocent. What this implies is not a necessarily symmetrical alternative of 'opacity' or 'guilt', but a textual entanglement. Like Wallace Stevens' Phosphor (a mask, I take it, for the poet as well as the reader, for they are indistinguishable) we read by the only light we possess, 'our own', a light not really distinguishable from the surrounding 'green night'; and it teaches 'a fusky alphabet'.

Caveat lector. If one of the conventions of the textual genre in which I am now writing is 'to attempt an objective exposition of significant developments in its field' (see preface, p. x), then it is a convention which puts the writer in a peculiarly defensive bind, when the impossibility of 'an objective exposition' is precisely the thing which she believes the field adumbrates. The gesture of mastery which an 'objective' order of reading desires to perform and consolidate has to struggle, as Hartman puts it, with a *'chaos of texts'*, and a chaotic verbal condition.

> Modern hermeneutics . . . is actually a negative hermeneutics. On its older function of saving the text, of tying it once again to the life of the mind, is superimposed the new one of doubting, by a parodistic or playful movement, master theories that claim to have overcome the past, the dead, the false. There is no Divine or Dialectical Science which can help us purify history absolutely, to pass in our lifetime a last judgment on it.
>
> (1976, 211–12)

Part I
Precursors

1

Richards revisited

> sure a poet is a sage;
> A humanist, Physician to all men.
>
> (Keats, *The Fall of Hyperion*)

It is often said that modern Anglo-American criticism begins
with the early work of I.A. Richards. This enabling fiction of a
'beginning' is conveniently located in *Principles of Literary
Criticism* (1924), the book which is at once the seminal
theorization of reader-oriented criticism and a brief for the
literary critical culture of the following decades. Yet *Principles
of Literary Criticism* is also in many respects the belated
culmination of Victorian earnestness, a redefinition of the
Arnoldian valorization of culture as the bulwark against
encroaching anarchy. Its message, informed by an urgent
vision of the value of art as a preparation for life, is
unequivocal. Poems are the unacknowledged legislators of
order, and poetry is a means of overcoming chaos; it will 'save
us' if we fulfil our responsibility of raising the standard of
response.

'The raising of the standard of response is as immediate a
problem as any, and the arts are the chief instruments by
which it may be raised *or lowered*' (1924, p. 234). Richards's
own emphasis on the threat of deteriorating response is
expressive of his acute sense not only of the ill-effects of poor
art and sub-culture, but also of the serious dangers accruing
from a decline in the quality and usefulness of our instruments
of communication, without which mutual understanding

between people(s) cannot take place. In the Ricardian defence of poetry, the role of the arts is very directly and intimately linked to the future welfare of humanity, for an understanding of the arts implies an understanding of the human mind. Such intelligence would enable the perfectibility of communication, response and, ultimately, of human action. On this point Richards is emphatic: what happens in the imaginative experience may modify all the rest of life:

> if we would understand the place of the arts in civilization we must consider them closely. An improvement of response is the only benefit which any one can receive, and the degradation, the lowering of a response, is the calamity.
>
> (p. 237)

Although the experience of art, for Richards, is definitely, even defiantly, continuous with the rest of our experience, it nevertheless remains a privileged category in his account. Art's peculiar virtue as an experience lies in the authorization of free mental *play*, empowering the untrammelled release of response which eventually resolves itself in a highly organized disposition of elements. The response to art achieves a completion rarely obtainable elsewhere. Experiences of art and play are, for better or worse,

> the most formative of experiences, because in them the development and systematisation of our impulses goes to the furthest lengths. In ordinary life a thousand considerations prohibit for most of us any complete working out of our response. . . . We have to jump to some rough and ready solution. But in the 'imaginative experience' these obstacles are removed. Thus what happens here, what precise stresses and preponderances, conflicts, resolutions and interinanimations, what remote relationships between different systems of impulses arise, what before unapprehended and inexecutable connections are established, is a matter which, we see clearly, may modify all the rest of life
>
> (pp. 237–8)

Ideally, the reading of poems is a privileged participation in the freedom of the imaginative experience. It leads to the practice of a fullness of response in other areas of experience.

We should read life, Richards is suggesting, as responsively, as fully and as freely as we read poems. And with response begins responsibility.

In retrospect, the centrality in Richards's writings of an abiding concern with language and the value of affect reveals an astonishing juncture of germinal (but also aborted) lines of inquiry which post-Ricardian theories of reading have engaged. Richards was a noble theoretician for all seasons, the extent of whose manifold interests cannot (and indeed, need not) be exhaustively represented here. I have therefore necessarily isolated for consideration only a few of those aspects which are instrumental in shaping this narrative, and which return as its leitmotiv.

Principles of literary criticism

The critic's foremost responsibility, as Richards perceived it in the early 1920s, was to clean up the verbal and philosophic situation in order to redefine the aesthetic realm and the aims of literary criticism.[1] His first projects, therefore, *Foundations of Aesthetics* (1921) and *The Meaning of Meaning* (1923), written in collaboration with C.K. Ogden, set out to map the territory where philosophy, linguistics, psychology and aesthetics meet. Then, impelled by the post-war sense of social and cultural crisis, he sought in *Principles of Literary Criticism* to foster a general revival of art, and to place aesthetics on a new footing adequate to the blunted sensibilities and epistemological uncertainties of a troubled twentieth century.

For a start, the issue of response was to be neither falsely aestheticized nor idealized. *The Meaning of Meaning* had argued that language is a system of signs and that an activity of *interpretation* underlies all thinking and communication. When interpretation is understood as 'a psychological reaction to a sign' then clearly the question of the reader's role must be engaged in other than the traditional categories which reify a 'phantom aesthetic state'. What Richards believed to be necessary was the rethinking of a theory of value and a theory of communication purged of all transcendental and metaphysical presuppositions.

Principles starts off with the task of demystifying the 'bogus entities' and 'hypostatized words' (p. 40) that had bedevilled antecedent projects of aesthetics in order to show that the value of art requires neither ethical nor metaphysical ideas for its justification. The 'aesthetic experience' *sui generis*, Richards argues, is a non-existent 'phantom'. Since all art is a mode of *experience*, no different in kind from any other mode of experience, the object of inquiry must be the work of the *mind*, as instrument of response and communication, rather than the work of *art* as sacrosanct, autonomous object.

> We are accustomed to say that a picture is beautiful, instead of saying that it causes an experience in us which is valuable in certain ways . . . we continually talk as though things possess certain qualities, when *what we ought to say* is that they cause effects in us of one kind or another [and] the fallacy of 'projecting' the effect and making it a quality of its cause tends to recur.
>
> (pp. 20–1, my emphasis).

To rid ourselves of this fallacy, the new theory of criticism must distinguish between what Richards calls *technical* remarks, which refer to the object, and *critical* remarks, which are about the value of the experience (p. 23). This position, far from being an appeal to subjectivity, is essentially anti-subjectivist; its purpose is to introduce and make possible a chastened and objective – one might even call it a pseudo-scientific – mode of critical discourse whose precision will be free of the impressionistic and subjectivist excesses of late-nineteenth-century writing.

But Richards evades the difficulties of the metalanguage to which he aspires by failing to determine its relationship to the object of study. The distinction between *technical* and *critical* remarks, for example, authorizes a separation between literary object and reading subject, a separation which the theory wishes to deny. It concedes the independent existence of a literary artefact about which *technical* remarks may be made, but also puts this independence in question by the appeal to *critical* remarks which are required to bring into being ('project') the literary artefact. This submerged ambiguity puts in doubt the 'objectivity' of the critical metalanguage and its concepts. The problem comes out into the open in

Richards's later work, which abandoned the hypothesis of neurophysiological causality to embrace a Coleridgean theory of mind, seeking to locate the epistemological moment in a coincidence or coalescence of an Object with a Subject. The act of knowing, in this view, is a kind of creation which 'makes no discoveries except in the sense of discovering what it has made' (*Coleridge On Imagination*, 1934, p. 49). As we shall see, it is frequently the inaugural gesture of contemporary reader-response criticisms to posit some version of this coalescence, but the nagging dualism of literary object and reading subject remains vexed. It continued to haunt Richards's relatively rare examples of close readings, and looms large in *Practical Criticism* (1929), the companion volume to *Principles*.

Indeed, Richards's early theory of communication cannot do without the duality. 'The two pillars upon which a theory of criticism must rest are an account of value and an account of communication' (1924, p. 23), he declared, for 'the arts are the supreme form of the communicative activity' (p. 26) as well as 'our storehouse of recorded values' (p. 32). In setting forth these twinned accounts, Richards negotiated an extremely precarious rhetorical balance between scepticism and idealism, between the determinate character of the literary object and the freedom of the reading subject, between the life of culture and the life of nature.

To begin with, his account of value is grounded in a reductive and dogmatized utilitarianism. 'What is good or valuable is the exercise of impulses and the satisfaction of their appetencies' (p. 58); anything that satisfies an appetency without frustrating some equal or more important appetency is valuable. Underlying this supposedly universal economy of balanced satisfaction and composure is Richards's unshakable conviction that 'our impulses must have some order, some organization or we do not live ten minutes without disaster' (1970, p. 40). Art is a supreme example of such 'order', and the value of art lies in its practical and theoretically quantifiable effects in organizing our minds; and even though 'we do not know enough yet about . . . that unimaginable organization, the mind, to say what order in any case actually exists, or between what the order holds', we do, nevertheless, 'know that a growing order is the principle of the mind' (1924, p. 50).

This principle, Richards claims, is most fully realized in works of art which organize the confusion that is experience. Experience itself is nothing other than an exposure to the pressures of a chaotic multitude of disorderly stimuli which find their most intricate and satisfying reconciliation in the mind of the artist who 'is the point at which the growth of the mind shows itself. . . . His work is the ordering of what in most minds is disordered' (p. 61). Richards believed that, provided we share a fund of common experience, the artist's product (poem, picture, piece of music) is undoubtedly, though perhaps never completely, communicable; not, of course, as strict transference or a participation in an identical experience, but as a transmissible paradigm of exemplary order. The recipient's experience of art in turn becomes a therapeutic reflection of/upon the metamorphosis from relative chaos to relative order, from confusion to a state of composed equilibrium.

Poetry is meliorative because it is a purveyor not of Truth or Beauty, but of mental health. A poem is not a *meaning* but a *means* of achieving an ordered balance and composure of impulses. Unlike the verbal structures of science, which point to things systematically and neutrally, the value of poems is neural: maximum cathexis combined with minimum frustration. Richards's notorious declaration that poems consist of 'pseudo-statements' was to outrage the New Critics by its denial of cognitive value to poetry, although they were not averse to the distinction between emotive and referential language from which it derives. In contrast to scientific statements, the statements of poetry are neither true nor false; they do not mediate knowledge, and their value is not measured by standards of verifiability or conformity to empirical facts, but by their psychological, therapeutic and civilizing effects. By extension, a poetic utterance is, for Richards, non-existent 'in itself'. Nor is literality or pure referentiality ever a feature of poetic discourse. Poems are always in a context, in a scene of 'interinanimation' – a word that Richards was particularly fond of repeating.

Geoffrey Hartman has aptly described Richards as a 'classicist of the nervous system' with decidedly romantic leanings towards a 'dream of communication' (1975, p. 30). Even in his early phase, Richards was a devout Coleridgean with respect to the doctrine of the Imagination as the faculty which reconstitutes the flux of our minds into an orderly cosmos. Paradoxically, this romantic faculty becomes the medium for the neoclassicist 'rage for order' that underwrites all Richards's theoretical speculations. But whether the Imagination is a property of the mind of its maker or the mind of its reader is a question over which Richards constantly shifts ground in *Principles*. Evidently his rudimentary and over-simplified theory of communication is not really distinguishable from his theory of value, and both theories converge in a mechanistic model of stimulus and response (see *Principles*, p. 116).

It is frequently claimed that Richards's thinking underwent an epistemological shift in the mid-1930s, away from positivism towards hermeneutics. Be that as it may, the later Richards[2] remains an evangelist of arduous reading, committed to the dialectical 'audit of meaning' (1955, p. 168), to the consonance and reciprocity of hermeneutic theory and practice, and to a renewed scrutiny of the symbolic machinery we construct to enable the acts of mediation we call comprehension. 'We must, if possible, gain some power of diagnosis, some understanding of the risks that interpretations run. . . . Sooner or later interpretation will have to be recognized as a key-subject. . . . We must make ourselves aware of how the language we so much depend upon works' (1929, pp. 315, 317, 319). He urges us to welcome rather than fear the instability of meaning; the anxiety of misunderstanding gives way to fresh speculation about the way 'words wander in many directions in [the] figurative space of meaning' (1955, p. 77).[3] That they do so 'systematically' is one of many casual Ricardian anticipations of later theory (the conduct of floating signifiers, for example) uttered well before post-Saussurean doctrines became a commonplace of our critical vocabularies.

The canonical precursor of New Critical doctrine is rarely remembered for his undoctrinaire essayistic reflections on the uncertainties of comprehension, and perhaps that is why today his parenthetical observations ('–it is worth recalling that grammar takes its name from writing –' (1936, p. 47)) spring into new prominence in a reading consciousness shaped by grammatology. His use of specialized quotation marks, for example, becomes in retrospect a precursive gesture of placing words if not quite under erasure then at least in a frame calculated to heighten consciousness of their problematic rhetorical functions. (For a concise summary of the types of quotation marks see Richards, 1970, pp. 100–4). Reading the mythologies of primitive peoples or of our own bourgeois culture like a language, constructing a post-Freudian psycho-aesthetics, reading the unconscious (also like a language), demystifying the figural or rhetorical structures of literary language are not projects that we trace directly to Richards. Refracted through New Critical borrowings, his name is indelibly associated with our most common working definition of metaphor as consisting of 'tenor' and 'vehicle'; with the orthodoxy of 'practical criticism'; with a distinction between emotive and referential language; and with many other household terms in the discourse of English Studies. This is partly due to Richards's own zeal in translating his heterodox ideas into operative pedagogical instruments. Nevertheless, the forgotten terms of his discussion of metaphor – the verbal phenomenon which, for Richards, was never a deviant or added power of language but rather its omnipresent principle and constitutive form (1936, p. 90) – are still vital. Metaphor, he also says parenthetically, is another name for what the psychoanalysts call 'transference' so that a 'command of metaphor' will go deep into 'the control of the world that we make for ourselves to live in' (p. 135). The New Critical appropriation of Richards as a precursor, his successors' adoption and adaptation of the more rigid technicalities offered as aids to practical criticism, effectively repressed this explicit equation of language with trope and its linkage with the life of the psyche, as it repressed or obscured other seminal but at the time unassimilable Ricardian ideas.

Practical criticism

What difference does theory make? Between the possession of ideas and their application, Richards noted shrewdly, there is a gulf. As in the act of interpretation, however much evidence we amass, we still have to jump to our conclusions.

Practical Criticism came into being as an attempt to explore and regulate the act of negotiating the gulf. Richards believed that 'critical principles . . . need wary handling. . . . Everything turns on how the principles are applied. It is to be feared that critical formulas, even the best, are responsible for more bad judgement than good' (pp. 10–11). The alarming prospect that the superiority of principles does not necessarily yield superior evaluations actually threatens to subvert the undertaking which this warning introduces. But Richards assumes that the threat can be controlled. 'Everything *turns* on *how* the principles are applied.' It is this 'turn' which largely generates the central ideas and strategies of *Practical Criticism* for bridging and unifying 'principles' and 'practice'. It also opens, as I hope to show, a critical division within Richards's project which subsequently enabled his New Critical followers to discard the principles whilst assimilating the practice of his theory of reading.

In point of historical fact, the New Critical investiture of method consigned *Practical Criticism* to the textbook shelf, thereby obscuring its legitimate place within the ranks of twentieth-century studies in what Richards called 'the natural history of human opinions and feelings' (p. 3).

> In part then this book is the record of *a piece of field work in comparative ideology*. But I hope, not only to present an instructive collection of contemporary opinions, presuppositions, theories, beliefs, responses and the rest, but also to make some suggestions towards a better control of these tricksy components of our lives.
>
> (p. 6, my emphasis)

It may be said that the procedure of *Practical Criticism* reverses that of its forerunner *Principles*. Here, theory (or at least a rule-governed process of interpretation) is empirically inferred from a pragmatic moment of (mis)reading. But the effect of this reversal is to challenge the validity of the founding principles (and in particular the theory of value and communication), blunting the cutting edge of their theoretical presuppositions with regard to the value of poetry as a freely engaged experience in the mind of the reader. The sometimes grotesque reading performances collected in part 2 of *Practical Criticism* – consisting of excerpts from students' interpretations of poems, counterpointed by Richards's own remarks on the performances – are a carnivalesque mockery of *Principles*.

The famous protocols experiment consisted of the following procedure: over a number of years, Richards issued his Cambridge audience of students with sheets of poems ranging from Shakespeare to Ella Wheeler Wilcox, upon which he requested them to 'comment freely'. 'The authorship of the poems was not revealed, and with rare exceptions it was not recognized' (p. 3). A 'reading' was defined as a number of perusals at one sitting, and some readers recorded as many as ten or twelve such readings, few giving less than four. Given the fact that the poems were not read cursorily, or that the protocol writers were not 'typical' readers of poetry but 'with few exceptions . . . the products of the most expensive kind of education' (p. 292), the results exhibit a thought-provoking and often dismal spectacle. Carelessness, self-indulgence and sentimentality are main vices; arrogance and obtuseness fall not far behind.

Richards attributes the shortcomings of his readers to their immaturity, their lack of 'general experience' and the defects of their education. It seems, though, that the ideological biases of the author of *Principles*, and the disingenuous invitation to 'comment freely', are also culpable in determining some of the embarrassment of raw response. 'I don't find this poem at all *helpful*', one student grumbles revealingly, 'nor does it express any feelings I have ever had or want to have' (p. 104). This is hardly surprising in the light of the scant preparation offered by *Principles* for a discriminating discourse *of* feelings and *about* feelings, and Richards should have realized that he had inadvertently bequeathed the licence to repress or ignore the referential and cognitive aspects, the 'plain sense' of the poems. Surely the idiosyncratic aberrations of the protocol writers were in part authorized and encouraged by an experiment whose theoretical presuppositions regarding the role and nature of 'feelings' in response were divided.

The intrusion of preconceptions and presuppositions is one of ten interlocking categories of 'difficulties' identified by Richards in his reading laboratory, although nothing is said about their inevitable entailment in the conditions of the experiment. The other difficulties, each analysed at length in part 3 of *Practical Criticism*, include failures to make out the 'plain sense' or to understand the poem both as statement and as expression; failures in 'sensuous apprehension' (the perception of form, movement, visual imagery); the intrusion of mnemonic irrelevances and stock responses; interferences in the economy of response caused by 'sentimentality' and its obverse 'inhibition'; the encroachment of ideological and doctrinal dissent or adhesion, technical presuppositions and general critical preconceptions. All these difficulties obstruct the channel of communication and the fullness of response. The underlying implication is that in some ideal situation of communication – given sufficient linguistic and literary competence, psychic poise, precise apprehension of tone and feelings, and an ability to order all these in due proportion – perfect understanding would ensue. Needless to say, the ideal scene of communication is not represented in the book. Its obverse – the persistent defectiveness of the communicative function – is the burden of Richards's text.

The great virtue of the 'protocols' of *Practical Criticism* lies in their capacity to provoke theoretical questions from within the empirical and pedagogical disarray which they so fully represent. Nevertheless, as I have suggested, a critical division inhabits the project from its inception. Its recommendations are a corollary of the hierarchy and segregation governing the relationship of principles and practice, but the book comes into being as an aid to performing the jump towards critical conclusions, to closing the gulf between 'technical' and 'critical' remarks. Although Richards never denies the discontinuity between these two levels, he masks the split between them by the production of a powerfully prescriptive method which conspires to create the appearance of an abridgement of theory and practice.

In a synoptic view Richards appears to be saying rather simplistically that poetry can, to be sure, be bewildering, but the real hindrance to its understanding does not lie in its essential difficulty; rather it is the reader who is being difficult. He must therefore be taught to read more carefully, and to transcend his idiosyncratic (neurotic or culture-bound) self, yet at the same time continue to recognize the self's 'genuine' experience as a 'touchstone for reality'.

The personal situation of the reader inevitably (and within limits rightly) affects his reading. . . . Though it has been fashionable – in deference to sundry confused doctrines of 'pure art' and 'impersonal emotions' – to deplore such a state of affairs, there is really no occasion. For a comparison of the feelings active in a poem with some personal feeling still present in the reader's lively recollection does give a standard, a test for reality. . . . Thus memories, whether of emotional crises or of scenes visited or incidents observed, are not to be hastily excluded as mere personal intrusions. That they are personal is nothing against them – all experience is personal – *the only conditions are that they must be genuine and relevant, and must respect the liberty and autonomy of the poem.*

(p. 277, my emphasis)

The habitual urbanity of Richards's style should not blind us to the double messages in a text teeming with concepts that ought to be placed within specialized quotation marks. Every assertion is hedged, and that which is expelled returns as the very condition of reading. Notable is the distinct Eliotic bias, despite disclaimers, expressed in the expectation that the reader dissociate himself from the bias of the 'personal' yet retain the 'genuine' content of experience which constitutes personality. The gesture of dividing the reader from his experience (including his reading) echoes Eliot's famous severance of the poem from its maker. 'Poetry is not a turning loose of emotion, but an escape from emotion; its is not the expression of personality, but an escape from personality.' But Eliot included a rider which perhaps not accidentally restores the banished term: 'of course, only those who have personality and emotions know what it means to want to escape from these things' (1932, p. 21). It is only by taking so much for granted (the nature of personality, the ontology of the subject, his authenticity or autonomy, etc.) that the standards for this equivocal admitting/dismissing of 'the personal situation of the reader' can be both predicated and evaded.

A double gesture of denial and assertion informs all the analyses of 'difficulties' in *Practical Criticism* but nowhere more suggestively or acutely than in the fifth chapter of part 3, the discussion of 'stock responses'. Again, the manifest gist is simple enough: stock responses – released by some particular memory of the reader's biography, an opinion giving rise to an irrelevant train of thoughts, an association with another poem, an obsession or hobby-horse – can intervene in our understanding of a poem by setting up an 'irrelevant' external and falsifying standard which distorts the meaning and obstructs the channel of communication. Yet in the elaboration of the argument Richards is ingeniously at pains to foreground the economic metaphor embedded in his discourse, and to make clear that stock responses are the very things which constitute the hermeneutic exchange or communicative channel.

> A stock response, like a stock line in shoes or hats, may be a convenience. Being ready-made, it is available with less trouble than if it had to be specially made out of raw or partially prepared materials. . . . Indeed, an extensive repertory of stock responses is a necessity. Few minds could prosper if they had to work out an original, 'made to measure' response to meet every situation that arose – their supplies of mental energy would be too soon exhausted and the wear and tear on their nervous systems would be too great. . . . But equally clearly there are in most lives fields of activity in which stock responses, if they intervene, are disadvantageous and even dangerous, because they may get in the way of, and prevent, a response more appropriate to the situation
>
> (p. 228)

Where can reading begin, Richards is saying, if not within a common-place, a public hermeneutic market? In engaging the tension between public and private Richards opens up significant new vistas, but he also retreats too soon from the consequences of his insights. If conventionalized reactions are at once the enabling and disabling agents in the interpretive exchange, then the significance and authority of stock responses as a means of situating reading must be rethought in terms of the public and social or institutional level, as well as – or better yet, in antithetical relation to – the private and psychological level. In the assertion that stock responses should not be barred, and that we should regard them as available 'energy systems' (p. 229) to draw on, Richards took an important but still-born step towards the recognition and re-examination of these phenomena not only as necessary crutches to assist the 'unsupported self' (p. 296) in its confrontation with the predicament of reading, but as the prerequisite of reading itself. Fifty years later the polarity of self and convention continues to chart the concerns of Anglo-American reader-oriented criticism, with critics such as Jonathan Culler and Stanley Fish, on the one hand, overinvesting the public pole by urging the idea that both poems and their interpretations are the products of institutionalized assent to certain strategies of reading; and Norman Holland and David Bleich, on the other hand, pursuing the 'characterological' and subjective aspects of interpretation.

Perhaps where Richards comes closest to what we recognize as modern criticism is not to be found in any one of his doctrines, but in the cultivation of a self-reflexive or self-interrogating moment which is both the cause and the effect of the close reading of literary texts. Throughout his writings there is a keen awareness that the authority of any order of reading crumbles without 'some understanding of the risks that interpretations run' (p. 315). A criticism alert to its own preconceptions, rather than eliciting 'a hundred verdicts from a hundred readers' (p. 172) or the 'mental inertia' (p. 295) of unthinking and automatic response, will encourage reflection on the nature of its own activity, and will thereby liberate itself from the restrictions of self on the one hand and of convention on the other. But even this liberating consciousness, in a truly dialectical audit, is not a fail-safe device, because *any* strategy of reading can be anaesthetized into an automatic repetition of itself. Richards's warning, that stock responses should be handled with care because 'the automatic, habitual interpretation steps in too quickly' (p. 229), applies equally to all reading strategies, and its validity does not stale. Perhaps no single method of response, he implies, will be adequate to the slow patient labour of interpretation or will contain the hazards. But Richards also wards off the impasse of interminable hesitation with the idealism of Good Sense. Certain kinds of response – the self-repeating, hobby-horsical or obsessional – must be banned lest the critic become an insufferable Uncle

Toby of interpretation. When all is said and done, he implies, masterly reading is the normative pursuit of an adjustment of interests and an abatement of differences.

Retrospective Richards

It is more than likely that I have read into Richards a self-interrogating stance which distorts his 'plain sense', but the dialectical audit, once set loose, is relentless. 'Fundamentally', says Richards, 'though this is an unfair way of putting it, when any person misreads a poem it is because, *as he is at that moment* he wants to' (1929, p. 229). But when is reading ever disinterested or free of history or desire? The cluster of genetic and economic questions released by the multi-purpose concept of 'stock' (questions of class, race and pedigree, capital and investment, supply and demand, institutionalized standards and opinions), recalls the intersection of interests which is the origin and destination of Richards's 'field work in comparative ideology' (p. 6). The Ricardian labour of freeing reading from difficulties often obscures this intersection, and when it is recalled the lightness of touch can easily mislead. 'Every interpretation is motivated by some interest, and the idea that appears is the sign of those interests that are its unseen masters' (p. 229). This is a sentence for semiologists, sociologists, hermeneuts and other readers to feast on. John Crowe Ransom, the New Critical godfather who despised Richards's psychologism, misread the metaphor weakly as a synonym for the 'appetencies' unfortunately celebrated in *Principles*: 'I suspect that Mr Richards' zeal on behalf of the little interests contains some pious fraud', Ransom sneered. 'His interests are going to be very tiny, very many and very private' (1938, p. 152). The pious fraud, however, may be Ransom's, who expends several rather anxiety-ridden pages on miniaturizing the 'little interests' into absurdity before he plays his etymological card and reads a little more closely. Interests, to be anything, he says, 'must be interests in external reality. *Inter-esse* means to be environed, and interest means sensitiveness to environment' (p. 155). Precisely: if anything, Richards should be read even more literally. The etymology of the word 'interest' – meaning to be between, to be different – points to the complex space of difference between public and private, external and interior, objective and subjective, where the struggle for possession and signification takes place. To be environed need not mean, as Ransom supposes, that within the environment is a central and choice piece of transcendental truth to be plucked. The space of difference is where meaning must be made.

My retrospective account of Richards takes an admittedly sceptical view of his pursuit of a golden civilizing mean monitoring standardization on the one hand and idiosyncrasy on the other. If I misinterpret his moral, pedagogical and evaluative Good Sense, however, that is as it should be, and Richards himself may be summoned to my defence. 'We must cease to regard misinterpretation as a mere unlucky accident. We must treat it as the normal and probable event' (p. 315). (Mis)interpreting Richards is a measure of how intellectually vital he remains, and is thus our highest tribute to the critic who more than any other is responsible, no matter how indirectly, for the way we read. Rereading Richards on the mind's capacity to renew and reorganize itself through the encounter with art teaches us that ultimately we earn our right to respond, not by the dogmatic application of a correct technique, but by practising a due respect for difference. The pleasure of rereading Richards lies in the discovery or recognition that he has anticipated us (the present generation of critics) by his own sensitivities to the divided core of critical writing.

'Nearly all good poetry is disconcerting . . .', Richards remarks finely at the end of his chapter on irrelevance and stock response. 'Some dear habit has to be abandoned if we are to follow it' (p. 240). It is the disconcerting (disjoining), endlessly absorbing otherness of poetry, with its resourceful and inherent opportunities for misunderstanding, that opens up a gulf for interpretation to bridge, a space for the reader to situate himself. What difference, then, does theory make? Very little, I would argue, if by theory we mean the small change of specific techniques or doctrines of comprehension or perfect communication. But when 'theory' is understood in its radically dramatic sense of speculation – a sustained and lively spectatorship at the scene of signification, a controlled reflection on an unfolding responsorium – then theory is that which makes the critical difference. It brings into consciousness the interval or interlude between ideas and their application. We do not solve problems by means of theory; only sort their components out differently. But that is where the action is, the play of meaning. Roland Barthes comments somewhere that 'theoretical' does not mean abstract; it means reflexive, something which turns back on itself. A discourse which turns back on itself is by virtue of this fact theoretical. In this sense *Practical Criticism* is a theoretical book of distinction, and an exemplar of the consonance and reciprocity of theory and practice. Everything turns not on the 'how' of application, but on the self-reflexive moment which is itself a turn away from the confidence of application.

2
New Criticism
and the avoidance of reading

The first law to be prescribed to criticism, if we may
assume such authority, is that it shall be objective,
shall cite the nature of the object rather than its
effects on the subject.

(J.C. Ransom, 'Criticism, Inc.')

New Criticism scarcely requires an introduction; it presents
itself, as Terence Hawkes allusively puts it, as 'criticism itself'
(1977, p. 152), our prevalent and remarkably tenacious mode
of literary analysis which regards the poem – the thing itself –
as an autonomous object to be examined in and on its own
terms. Roughly from the mid-1930s to the late 1950s (1957,
which saw the publication of Northrop Frye's *Anatomy of
Criticism*, seems a reasonable *terminus ad quem*) the shape of
English studies was changed and consolidated by the work of a
number of leading American critics profoundly stimulated by
the ideas I.A. Richards and T.S. Eliot had put into circulation.
The writings of John Crowe Ransom, Allen Tate, R.P. Blackmur, Cleanth Brooks, René Wellek, W.K. Wimsatt and others
represent the powerful movement which came to be known as
the New Criticism and which made rapid inroads into the
academy. Though hardly homogeneous, the group is generally
associated with doctrines of the text's objectivity, its self-
sufficiency and 'organic unity'; with a formalist, 'intrinsic'
approach to the text; with a resistance to paraphrase and to

the separation of form and content; and above all with the technique of 'close reading' – a mode of exegesis that pays scrupulous attention to the rich complexity of textual meaning rendered through the rhetorical devices of irony, ambiguity and paradox.

Intellectual movements are not created *ex nihilo*, but their incorporation of precursors can take strange turns. J.C. Ransom copiously and repeatedly took Richards to task for saying that the use of poetry is psychological and emotive rather than cognitive and disinterested, and his chapter on Richards in the book *The New Criticism* (1941), which gave the movement its name, offers a laborious critique of Richards's *Principles of Literary Criticism*. Yet it begins by announcing that 'the new criticism very nearly began with him' (p. 3), and concludes by identifying the movement with the work of Richards and his brilliant disciple, William Empson. Of the new style of literary exegesis Ransom writes that

> writings as acute and at the same time as patient and consecutive as this have not existed in English criticism, I think, before Richards and Empson. They become frequent now; Richards and Empson have spread quickly. That is a principal reason why I think it is time to identify a powerful intellectual movement that deserves to be called a new criticism.
>
> (p. 111)

It is ironic but perhaps not accidental that reader-response criticism very nearly came into being with the New Criticism. Inasmuch as it didn't, and Richards's inaugural theorization of the question of reading suffered a long hiatus during the New Critical heyday, an excursus on the New Critics would seem to be an irrelevant digression. Whereas reader-response criticisms variously dismiss the objective existence of the text and emphasize the primacy of the reader or the act of reading in the constitution of literary meaning and value, the New Critics rejected the reader together with 'subjectivistic' and psychological theories of value. Yet in a sense which I hope this chapter will illuminate, it is the strikingly indecisive marginalization of the reader which makes the New Critical phase so pertinent to our story for, notwithstanding theoretical manifestos to the contrary, an overwhelming but suppressed or rarely acknowledged concern with the reader was at the heart of the New Critical project. Despite its ostensible endeavours to hypostatize the objectivity or autonomy of the literary work, the ghostly presence of 'readers' enacts a continuing resistance to its own dicta from within the project itself.

New Criticism managed to retain almost intact the Ricardian principles of organization and balanced order and the reconciliation of contending impulses by simply transferring the mechanism of resolution and equilibrium from the reader's mind to the verbal structure of the poem. As a principle intrinsic to the text, the drama of thrust and counterthrust, tension and resolution enacted in the figures of irony, paradox and ambiguity, both provided the basis for an 'objective' rhetorical description of the literary work and also generated the theory and methodology of close reading. But although the selective appropriation and accommodation of Ricardian notions had the outcome of effectively bringing to a halt the development of reader-response theory, the massive espousal of Richards's terms left a persistent residue, and the reader, banished by doctrinal fiat, refused to be entirely dislodged by the concerted New Critical effort to objectify the literary work of art. If Richards begat the enemy brothers of reader-response criticism and 'objective' formalist criticism at once, the trace of that common root may go some way towards explaining some of the resemblances as well as the inner contradictions which beset these rival programmes.

How this came to be, how New Critical rhetoric betrays its own self-division, the ways in which the detour of New Criticism may be seen to play a significant, albeit oblique and negative, role in cultivating what was in effect a suppressed and unacknowledged reader-oriented criticism – these and related matters will be the concern of the following pages.

Regulating and deregulating meaning: Richards and Empson

In *Practical Criticism* Richards had made the question of meaning his diagnostic starting point on the axiomatic assumption that the literary text, like all language, is an intelligible signifying system, that its meaning is precise and communicable, and that 'the all-important fact for the study of literature – or any other mode of communication – is that there are several kinds of meaning' (1929, p. 173).

It was his authentic respect for semantic instability and for the prodigality of verbal meaning, joined with his belief in the perfectibility of communication that bred Richards's aspiration to analyse, institutionalize and thereby curb a seemingly uncontrollable proliferation of idiosyncratic readings. But as so often with Richards, antithetical impulses inform his programme. Having deregulated the norms governing aesthetic response by electing the authority of a constituting subject, Richards proceeded to install qualifying and supplementary regulations and constraints intended to revoke the excesses of subjectivity and restore both textual and authorial prerogatives for the determination of meaning. Throughout *Practical Criticism* the implication is that the reader's task is to construe the correct meaning inserted by an author into his text; the variability of meaning (Richards speaks of 'several *kinds*') refers, therefore, neither to the reader's subjectivity nor to the indeterminacy of language – the rebellious phenomenon of semantic plurality of the kind which Empson explored – but rather to a set of identifiable functions of linguistic usage, a regulated instrumentality of language.

Specifying the kinds of meaning or the functions of verbal behaviour can become a mystifying numerological exercise. One can easily begin with the claim that meaning is fundamentally of *two* kinds, subjective (an interpretive act) or objective (a textual fact). Richards himself put in circulation the distinction between emotive and referential uses of language. Communication theory, however, postulates a *three*-fold scheme of mediation in which the elements of a *message* sent by an *addresser* to an *addressee* have three corresponding linguistic functions reflecting the referential, the emotive or expressive, and the conative or affective origins of meaning respectively. That Richards divided meaning into *four* kinds or aspects (which he named Sense, Feeling, Tone, and Intention), seems to be no more of a logical necessity than Empson's distribution of ambiguity into *seven* kinds, although the talismanic number is not without allusive or figurative resonance. (I detect an oblique reference to metaphysical and hierarchical schemes such as the medieval four-fold system of exegesis; perhaps the puzzling *four* is Richards's witty reminder that his is a distinctly temporal, secular and egalitarian ideal of understanding.) As hermeneutic aids, however, the differences between the categories of *Sense* ('we use words to direct our hearers' attention upon some state of affairs'), *Feeling* ('attitude . . . bias or accentuation of interest . . . some personal flavour'), *Tone* ('an attitude to [the] listener') and *Intention* ('the effect he is endeavouring to promote' (pp. 175–6)) are extremely tenuous. There is a disorienting overlap and the four kinds all partake of some mixture of the referential, the expressive and the affective poles of communication. (To his discussion of *Intention* Richards adds a bewildered footnote admitting that 'this function is plainly not on all fours [!] with the others' (p. 176) and then refers us to a corrective appendix which only compounds the confusion.) Ultimately the aspects collapse into each other; even *Sense*, presumably a purely referential aspect of language, is not free of feeling or intention in Richards's definition: 'we use words', he says, 'to direct our hearers' attention . . . to present to them . . . to excite in them . . .' (p. 175). In the strain to locate the signifying function sometimes in language itself and sometimes in consciousness, Richards's determinants of literary meaning become obstinately indeterminate.[1] This equivocation puts in question the basic presupposition (adopted by the New Criticism) that language has a stable signifying force, that it means what it says and says what it means, and that what it communicates, in the last analysis, is the complexity of experience.

The assumption of a communicable continuity between signifier and signified is put to the test when it encounters the impasse of conflicting and irreconcilable interpretations which reading educes. William Empson's *Seven Types of Ambiguity* (1961, first published 1930), inspired by Richards's tutelage, inadvertently illustrates this impasse by raising the floodgates of meaning. His pioneering scrutiny of 'any *verbal nuance*, however slight, which gives room for *alternative reactions* to the same piece of language' (p. 1, my emphasis) seeks to analyse the ways in which a statement can be effective or meaningful in several ways at once, and is a brilliantly original exercise in putting hermeneutic pressure on fragments of literary text, teasing out the 'echoes and recesses' (p. 199) of words, and tracing the directions in which they wander to constitute the figurative space of meaning. Here is a frequently quoted example:

> The fundamental situation, whether it deserves to be called ambiguous or not, is that a word or a grammatical structure is effective in several ways at once. To take a famous example, there is no pun, double syntax, or dubiety of feeling, in
>
> Bare ruined choirs, where late the sweet birds sang,
>
> but the comparison holds for many reasons; because ruined monastery choirs are places in which to sing, because they involve sitting in a row, because they are made of wood, are carved into knots and so forth, because they used to be surrounded by a sheltering building crystallised out of the likeness of a forest, and coloured with stained glass and painting like flowers and leaves, because they are now abandoned by all but the grey walls coloured like the skies of winter, because the cold and Narcissistic charm suggested by choir-boys suits well with Shakespeare's feeling for the object of the Sonnets, and for various sociological and historical reasons (the protestant destruction of monasteries; fear of puritanism) which it would be hard now to trace out in their proportions; these reasons, and many more relating the simile to its place in the Sonnet, must all combine to give the line its beauty, and there is a sort of ambiguity in not knowing which of them to hold most clearly in mind. Clearly this is involved in all such richness and heightening of effect, and the machinations of ambiguity are among the very roots of poetry.
>
> (pp. 2–3)

It might seem that the effectiveness of Shakespeare's structure of figurations in Sonnet 73, where the experience of old age and declining powers (including poetic powers) is imaged by wintry trees (the latter end of the seasons of life), in turn imaged by bare ruined choirs (the absence of song), may be intuited without difficulty. But an analysis of the figurative yield of the verbal fragment, as in Empson's commentary, yields far more than this sensible intuitive response requires or can support. The consequent indeterminacy of meaning raises the question of the intellectual responsibility of *too much* critical interpretation. 'Irresponsible criticism' was F.W. Bateson's curt judgement of Empson's procedure, when he argued that a modicum of historical knowledge and, above all, reference to the verbal context would determine the irrelevance of most of these associations (1950, p. 180). The question that arises therefore is what and where are the limits of response? Can or should such limits be drawn? What is to prevent the reader from riding roughshod across the boundaries of common sense and performing 'irresponsible' criticism? What risks does Empson's reading method run, and what consequences follow?

It has been pointed out more than once that Empson's use of the term 'ambiguity' is confusingly loose and that what he is surveying is types of multiple meaning which are not necessarily of the order of disjunctiveness proper to a strict notion of ambiguity (see Rimmon-Kenan 1977, pp. 16–26). But what is more pertinent to our survey is the manner in which Empson assumes yet shirks the 'onus of reconciliation' placed on the reader (p. 193, n. 1). The relationship between 'verbal nuance' and 'alternative reactions' is left deliberately vague, and it is on the consequences of this vagueness that I wish to focus. Like Richards, Empson chooses to bracket the problem of deciding whether the phenomenon of ambiguity is a property of language or of response. Early on in the book he notes the ambiguity of 'ambiguity' in this respect, only to dismiss the problem casually:

> 'Ambiguity' itself can mean an indecision as to what you mean, an intention to mean several things, a probability that one or other or both of two things has been meant, and the fact that a statement has several meanings. It is useful to be able to separate these if you wish, but it is not obvious that in separating them at any particular point you will not be raising more problems than you solve. Thus I shall often use the ambiguity of 'ambiguity', and pronouns like 'one', to make statements covering both reader and author of a

poem, when I want to avoid raising irrelevant problems as
to communication.

(pp. 5–6)

That the problems are both complicated and relevant in the
highest degree, and that communication itself is at stake, has
been the burden of all theories of reading.

In an important critique of Richards and Empson, Paul de
Man pointed out that if the underlying expectation in the
analysis of figurative language is an adequation between the
figure and the experience figured, then the adequacy or mimetic
force of the comparison (old age is like wintry boughs which
are like bare ruined choirs) is undone by its deployment of the
initial experience (old age) 'into an infinity of associated experiences that spring from it'. Instead of fixing the originary
experience, metaphor leads to 'a dizziness of the mind'. Far
from referring back to an object that would be its cause, 'the
poetic sign sets in motion an imaging activity that refers to no
object in particular. The "meaning" of the metaphor is that
it does not "mean" in any definite manner' (1983, p. 235).
What has become indeterminate is precisely the relationship
between a hypostatized original experience (the author's, let
us say, presumably placed *in* the text) and the reader's ex-
trapolation of that experience (presumably triggered by the
text). Giving free rein to the poetic sign puts at risk the very
possibility of communication.

Empson finds himself face to face with this risk at the
extreme end of the scale (the seventh type) of ambiguity, in
which 'the two meanings of the word, the two values of the
ambiguity, are the opposite meanings defined by the context',
but retreats from the danger of indeterminacy by suggesting
that 'the total effect is to show a fundamental division in the
writer's mind'. This rather weak piece of psychologism is
countered by the following remarkably resonant reflection upon
the way language works:

> A contradiction of this kind may be meaningless, but can
> never be a blank; it has at least stated the subject which is
> under discussion, and has given a sort of intensity to it such
> as one finds in a gridiron pattern in architecture because
> it gives prominence neither to the horizontals nor to the

verticals, and in a check pattern because neither colour is the ground on which the other is placed; it is at once an indecision and a structure, like the symbol of the Cross.

(p. 192)

What is remarkable is the knot of so many post-structural issues anticipated by this uncanny sentence. In the first instance the radicalization of ambiguity in Empson's seventh type hovers on the verge of acknowledging that indeterminacy of meaning characterizes poetic language. The signifying values of a structure of undecidability, oscillating between figure and ground, can no longer be settled by an appeal to the formal properties of the text which, in being at once itself and other to itself, cannot resolve its own contradictions; it can only, to borrow de Man's word, 'name' them (p. 237). The text has become unreadable in the sense that it is unable to say its originary experience, but can only communicate its indeterminacy. Empson's evasion of his own insight, by reducing the verbal uncertainty to a reflection of division in the author's mind, will not stand up to scrutiny for, on his own terms, the text's representational or mimetic power is reduced to only one mode of signification: an arbitrary bewilderment. Ambiguity has become more than a contradiction; it is the condition which undermines the text's power to transmit a complex meaning or to represent any experience except the experience of its own divisiveness and unreadability.

If this is indeed the case, we are now in a position to perceive that the seventh type of ambiguity is not essentially different from the case of Empson's first example of 'bare ruined choirs'. There the numerous meanings evoked were said to 'combine', and ambiguity was a condition of the reader's response – 'not knowing which of them to hold most clearly in mind'. Combination, no less than the failure to combine, rests with the reader. If in a sufficiently extended sense (a sense to which Empson subscribes) all literary language is 'ambiguous', i.e. indeterminate, then the differences between type seven and type one are only minor differences of degree – both types being subject to the same structure of understanding – so that the question of the mediating, constitutive role of a reader returns with renewed urgency. Empson's belief that any contradiction is likely to have some sensible interpretation contriving the association of opposites reinforces the need to assign a role to the reader. Yet on this issue Empson remains at his most characteristically New Critical: he recoils from the possible breakdown of a formalist view of the text as an objective 'piece of language'. His retreat from the edge of the abyss of indeterminacy and unreadability to which his theory of the text's ambiguity has led, and his reluctance to engage with psychological criteria or any other reader-response theory, are inscribed in a footnote which gives some indication of how far afield Empson's speculations were willing to roam, yet also betrays an entire tradition's proclivity for Good Sense joined to a distaste for theorizing and philosophizing:

> It may be said that the contradiction must somehow form a larger unity if the final effect is to be satisfying. But the onus of reconciliation can be laid very heavily on the receiving end. One could, of course, also introduce much philosophical puzzling about the reconciliation of contradictions. The German tradition in the matter seems eventually based on Indian ideas, best worked out in Buddhism. But I daresay there is more than enough theorizing in the text here already.
>
> (p. 193, n. 1)

The ontological shift: 'A poem should not mean but be'

The anti-affective stance of New Criticism was the major, uneasy swerve away from the founding father. Richards's early epistemological position, as we saw, postulated that the world or the text are known to us insofar as they are constituted by the mind; the work of literary art is an event in the mind of a reader, a structure of response or consciousness which recreates an original moment of composure achieved by the poet and rendered in his poem. 'It is never what a poem says which matters', Richards declared, 'but what it is' (1970, p. 33). This 'ontological' assertion grew out of his profound concern with the declining status of art, the very concern which led him to shift the grounds of the discussion away from the object to its psychological effects. For Richards the poem was identified

with and defined by an experience of considerable psychological value, but was not granted any objective or inherent
cognitive content.

It was over the issue of what a poem is rather than how to
read it that the New Critics disagreed with Richards. For
them, poetry was a rival mode of knowledge to science, a mode
whose intelligibility depended upon objectivity. They believed
that literature tells its own truths and possesses its own cognitive
freight; that the literary object should be understood not neurally
but neutrally; and that interpretation should therefore appeal
neither to the writer's intention nor to a reader's response but
to a description of the thing itself. For J.C. Ransom the intent
of the good critic must be 'to examine and define the poem with
respect to its structure and texture' but 'the final desideratum
is an ontological insight'. This is, he writes, 'in the last resort, a
speculative exercise' – and the word 'speculative' (from the
Latin for mirror) must be allowed its full implications – 'but
my secret committal was to speculative in the complete sense
of – ontological' ('Criticism as pure speculation', first published
1941, in Adams 1971, p. 887). Perhaps Ransom's ironic style of
reflection softens the aggressive repudiation of psychology in
favour of the metaphysics of the self-sufficient text, but his
purpose is clear. If epistemology – the mode of knowing – is
bracketed, on the disarming assumption that meaning will
empirically take care of itself, then the ontological shift can be
presented almost fatalistically: 'the critic will doubtless work
empirically and set up his philosophy only as the drift of his
findings will compel him. But ultimately he will be compelled.
He will have to subscribe to an ontology' (p. 890).

The tacit understanding behind this move is that the
ontological question – what is a poem? – can be decided by
simply taking the epistemological question – how do we know?
– for granted; that is to say, as already settled on empirical
grounds. But this move avoids, even as it uses, the intercon-
nectedness of the epistemological and ontological questions.
Crudely put, the ontological dilemma of post-Kantian literary
theorizing is the following: there is no 'object' out there unless
we extrapolate it from our 'experience' of knowing; once
extrapolated, the object becomes the enabling and controlling
feature of our experience of knowing. This indissoluble

continuity between epistemology and ontology undermines any sharp distinction or separation between knower and known, and produces the seamless circularity which Murray Krieger names the 'metaphysical pathos' of literary theory: 'we must face the need to have some common residue we can refer to as the work, even though we know how hard it is to get around ourselves to point to it' (1976, pp. 55, 48).

The interlocking nature of the epistemological and ontological questions, and the dialectical twisting of the strands of reader and text, represent the Gordian knot which New Criticism believed it could cut in order to pave the way for an autonomous 'literary scholarship'. And cut it they did, to establish the longest-lived Anglo-American critical hegemony of this century. But despite their resolution to construct a total and objective theory of literature the knot stubbornly resisted dissolution. Ironically enough, the remarkable success of New Criticism consisted in its rapid transformation into an *organon* of reading practices which repeatedly appealed to the mind of a 'reader' whilst assiduously avoiding the theoretical questions raised by its own performance.

This avoidance of the question of reading is one more telltale piece of evidence in what seems to be a systematic discrepancy or incongruity between theoretical precepts and the reading practices which they yield, or which yield them. Yet such discrepancies within discourse can generate a fertile dialectic of 'blindness and insight' (de Man 1983) whereby the insights of a critical project positively thrive on its moment of blindness. In the instance of New Criticism, the major theoretical difficulty – the problem of where to locate and how to account for literary meaning – yielded a considerable harvest of subtle interpretations, which in turn have become the impulse for new theoretical speculation.

'The defeat of the poem': Brooks and Warren

The direct effects of the 'ontological' shift are perhaps best reflected in the work of Cleanth Brooks and R.P. Warren who collaborated in transposing theoretical speculations into accessible pedagogical terms for the reading and analysis of individual poems. Their well-known textbooks, *Understanding*

Poetry (1938) and *Understanding Fiction* (1943), went through numerous editions and served more than any other New Critical writing to disseminate the new methodology of 'close reading'. Another influential text, Brooks's propaedeutic *The Well-Wrought Urn* (1947), which contains elaborate interpretations of major poems in the English canon, is a subtle and sophisticated demonstration of the principle that 'poems were to be read as one has learned to read Donne and the moderns' (p. 193). It is not difficult to detect the undertow of metaphysical pathos underwriting Brooks's reading strategies. To read on the assumption that the language of poetry is always the language of paradox and irony is, of course, to elide the history of culture and of literary styles, reducing all literature to a single synchronic system governed by the same universal rhetorical principles. But even if we make allowances by putting aside, for the moment, the evasion of literary history, there still remains in Brooks's theory of reading the question of a persistent equivocation between the text – the timeless thing in itself – and its temporal realizations in the act of reading.

The informing premises underlying Brooks's reading strategy are conveniently set forth in one of the concluding chapters of *The Well-Wrought Urn* entitled 'The heresy of paraphrase'. The poem is not a 'paraphrasable core' of meaning but a 'structure' which assembles and orders all the materials of the poem. 'The nature of the material sets the problem to be solved, and the solution is the ordering of the material' (p. 194). Poems, for Brooks, are nothing so much as challenges to the wit of the reader, complicated enigmas made of semantic and rhetorical paradoxes, ironies and ambiguities to be mastered by the act of reading and resolved into their essential 'unity'. Brooks treats this key concept gingerly; the unity of the structure, he writes, consists in 'balancing and harmonizing connotations, attitudes and meanings. . . . It unites like with unlike . . . not . . . however, by a simple process of allowing one connotation to cancel out another. . . . It is a positive unity, not a negative; it represents not a residue but an achieved harmony' (p. 195). Note how careful Brooks is to avoid an identification of 'unity' with 'meaning' – the unity resides in the structure, whereas meaning is presumably made by the reader; yet the reader is expected to extrapolate the meaning in terms of the poem's unity, its representation of achieved harmony. This unity, Brooks continues, is not paraphrasable. A poem resists paraphrase because it is not a statement that is true or false, but – like painting or music or architecture – it is a pattern of resolved stresses, or – like drama – an action, not a statement about action. No paraphrase can constitute the real core of meaning because the poem itself sets up a resistance to the meanings it provokes. 'Whichever alternative we take, there are elaborate qualifications to be made' (p. 197). Propositions about what the poem 'says' are only pragmatic working hypotheses. They are like temporary scaffolding thrown about a building; 'we must not mistake them for the internal and essential structure of the building itself' (p. 199). The implication is that the ontological X – the internal and essential thing itself – which the experience of reading will compel us to postulate will always elude us.

The obvious equivocation between ontology and epistemology typifies Brooks's elaborations of the ubiquitous concept of irony. In the 1949 essay entitled 'Irony as a principle of structure' (Brooks 1951) Brooks argues that irony is an acknowledgement of the pressures of context, which is to say that each part of a poem is modified by the whole. Any statement in a poem will possess an ironic potential, will show 'a qualification of the context' (p. 731), making the poem vulnerable to the warping and destabilizing effects of irony. This dynamic machinery, however, is governable, and it comes to a stop or reaches a stability of context when the internal pressures balance and mutually support each other. There is a point, Brooks argues, at which thrust and counterthrust cease to be subversive of each other and become the means of stability. An equilibrium is reached like the equilibrium of an arch: 'the very forces which are calculated to drag the stones to the ground actually provide the principle of support' (p. 733). The poem 'fuses' the irrelevant or discordant pressures, 'comes to terms with itself' and effectively becomes invulnerable to irony. 'Irony, then, in his further sense, is not only an acknowledgement of the pressures of a context. Invulnerability to irony is the stability of a context' (p. 732). How a poem can be both ironic and beyond irony is an assertion which must remain an open question, one which renders Brooks's own text vulnerable to the warping effects of irony.

The ideal of 'balanced poise, stable through its power of inclusion, not through the force of its exclusions' comes straight out of Richards (1924, p. 248), who pointed out that 'irony . . . consists in the bringing in of the opposite, the complementary impulses' (p. 250). But whereas for Richards irony is a mental experience ('the balance is not in the structure of the stimulating object [but] in the response' (p. 248)), for Brooks (as for Empson) irony is (or wants to be) an aspect of objective structure – a relationship between opposite but equally tenable parts of a poem – which generates the meaning and tone of the poem. We can clearly see here how uneasy lies the head that entertains the New Critical shift from mind to text, from consciousness to structure. On the one hand, Brooks rescues the term irony from its classical rhetorical status (a determinate trope of inversion, saying one thing and meaning another) by stretching its denotation far beyond the bounds of the traditional sense to include paradoxical (*para* – going against, *doxa* – received opinion) *effects* of indeterminacy and suspension of judgement arising from the act of reading. The consequent interpretive hesitation ought to alert us to the difficulties of describing irony in spatial formalistic terms. But Brooks, just like Empson when confronted with the consequences of radical ambiguity, recoils and urges the issue back to a formalism that will ensure the stability of the text and lead to interpretive closure. Indeterminacy of meaning, infinite negativity, disruptive subjectivity – all these had to be embargoed, as Hartman points out, to assure the poem's intelligibility and the critic's mastery. To keep irony 'practical' and tame, the New Critics reduced 'its strange, featureless, even daimonic flexibility (able to assume any shape) . . . to the status of serviceable Elf or Kobalt, the kind that helps poor shoemakers cobble shoes as long as no one tries to catch spirit in the act' (1980, p. 278).

A strikingly undomesticated incarnation of Hartman's whimsical metaphor occurs in R.P. Warren's well-known account of the reconciliation of opposites which the successful poem enacts. The essay 'Pure and impure poetry', first published in 1943, repeatedly betrays the exasperating strain which the concept of irony places on the separation of reader and text. It begins with the admission that no one strategy of reading will quite work 'the defeat of the poem'.

> For the poem is like the monstrous Orillo in Boiardo's *Orlando Inamorato*. When the sword lops off any member of the monster, that member is immediately rejoined to the body, and the monster is as formidable as ever. But the poem is even more formidable than the monster, for Orillo's adversary finally gained a victory by an astonishing feat of dexterity: he slashed off both the monster's arms and quick as a wink seized and flung them into the river. The critic who vaingloriously trusts his method to account for the poem, to exhaust the poem, is trying to emulate this dexterity: he thinks that he, too, can win by throwing the lopped-off arms into the river. But he is doomed to failure. . . . There is only one way to conquer the monster: you must eat it, bones, blood, skin, pelt and gristle. And even then the monster is not dead, for it lives in you, is assimilated into you, and you are different, and somewhat monstrous yourself for having eaten it.
>
> So the monster will always win, and the critic knows this. He does not want to win. He knows that he must always play stooge to the monster. All he wants to do is to give the monster – the poem – a chance to exhibit again its miraculous power, which is poetry
>
> (1958, p. 3)

This wonderful and disconcerting allegory of New Critical reading, with its inescapable moral – that a poem's mysterious otherness is unassailable and invincible unless we appropriate it by a violent act of mastery and incorporation – prefaces an otherwise entirely doctrinaire New Critical position along the lines of Brooks's theory of irony.

In Warren's view every poem is a self-contained system of 'resistances and tensions' held together in a single structure which, in order to 'succeed', must resolve and reconcile contradictory elements. The poet who wishes, for example, to represent a 'soft' subject such as romantic love must earn his right to engage our interest in his 'vision' by indicating that his subject can survive the complexities and contradictions of 'experience' by assimilating the hard counter-spirit of 'realism, wit, intellectual complication'. The poetic 'purity' of Romeo and Juliet's moonlight tryst is of a more complex kind than Tennyson's 'Now sleeps the crimson petal' or Shelley's 'The Indian Serenade' (a poem treated most unfavourably in *Understanding Poetry*) because it must coexist with the ironic counterpoint of an 'impure', tough, prosaic style; Mercutio's scepticism or the Nurse's bawdy jokes are 'the voice[s] of prose and imperfection' contaminating the Capulet garden, and they resist, contradict and complicate the thrust of the purely romantic experience represented by the lovers' scene. In short, Warren warns us that impure poetry (i.e. 'good' poetry) is not for the mind that is 'hot for certainties' (p. 31). But what are the consequences of coming to terms with Mercutio if not the establishment of a 'certainty', a conclusive defeat of the Mercutio element?

It is revealing that on the question of who or what does the reconciling Warren shifts ground in a series of vivid and inconclusive metaphors of strain and violence which tell a different, subterranean story:

> the poet is like the jiujitsu expert; he wins by utilizing the resistance of his opponent – the materials of the poem. In other words, a poem, to be good, must earn itself. It is a motion toward a point of rest, but if it is not a resisted motion, it is motion of no consequence. For example, a poem which depends upon stock materials and stock response is simply a toboggan slide, or a fall through space. And the good poem must, in some way involve the resistances; it must carry something of the context of its own creation; it must come to terms with Mercutio.
>
> (p. 27)

Not only are poem, poet and reader locked in combat, but each is at strife with his own identity. The critic wishes to defeat the monster-text, but he 'does not want to win'. The poet too desires to be master of his own poem, and the poem itself is represented as aspiring to its fragile and uncertain self-possession despite 'resistances'.

The upshot seems to be that New Critical poetics, like 'pure poetry', would like to be all of a piece, but finds itself divided by the presence of too many contestants for the authority of meaning. In his rage for reconciliation, Warren prevaricates over the question whether Mercutio is defeated by his creator, his verbal context, or by the reader. Coming to terms with Mercutio, he says, is 'another way of saying that a good poem involves the participation of the reader; it must, as Coleridge puts it, make the reader into "an active creative being"' (p. 27). But to invoke Coleridge is to repeat the basic indecisiveness with respect to the subject/object conundrum. As Ransom's fellow New Critic, Allen Tate, observed, Coleridge *'cannot make up his mind whether the specifically poetic element is an objective feature of the poem, or is distinguishable only as a subjective effect.* He cannot in short, choose between metaphysics and psychology' (1968, first published 1941, p. 95). Neither could the New Critics. By and large they clung to the omnibus notion of structure as 'dramatic', in the belief that the concept of drama self-evidently reconciles reified objective forms with subjective consciousness. Indeed, throughout New Critical discourse, temporal and dynamic terms (the poem as experience, as a mode of action, a drama or gesture) vie indiscriminately with spatial metaphors (the poem as verbal icon, well-wrought urn, a building or a structure). But the urge to inclusiveness stretches the concept of 'structure' to breaking point. The attempt to totalize the aesthetic experience by the super-imposition of a temporal act of understanding on the spatial metaphor of structure subverts the idea of stable form since 'form is never anything but a process on the way to its completion. The completed form never exists as a concrete aspect of the work' (de Man 1983, p. 31). New Critical discourse frequently implied but refused to acknowledge that the literary object comes into being through the act of under-standing. When epistemology threatened to undo ontology, their discourse suffered a failure of nerve, and a stiffening into dogma.

'Battering the object'

It should by now be amply clear why, despite the fact that New Criticism is commonly identified with the technique of 'close reading', the index to its major gospel, Wellek and Warren's *Theory of Literature* (1956, first published 1949), makes no mention of the reader and lists not more than two brief references to the item 'reading'. The first refers us to the 'reading public', a concern 'extrinsic' to the study of literature proper; the second is to be found in the concluding paragraph of the opening chapter in which the authors outline the necessity to distinguish between literature ('creative, an art') and literary study ('a species of knowledge or learning'). The overriding foundational goal of literary scholarship, they claim, is an *organon* of methods which, though different from the methods of science, will emulate the prestige of 'valid methods of knowing' (p. 5).

> To say that literary study serves only the art of reading is to misconceive the ideal of organized knowledge, however indispensable this art may be to the student of literature. Even though 'reading' be used broadly enough to include critical understanding and sensibility, the art of reading is an ideal for a purely personal cultivation. As such it is highly desirable, and also serves as a basis of a widely spread literary culture. It cannot, however, replace the conception of 'literary scholarship', conceived of as super-personal tradition.
>
> (pp. 7–8)

This peremptory suppression of the reading subject in the interests of an objective and intellectually valid discipline such as the New Critics aspired to was, as we saw, a key swerve away from the critical positions of Richards. If criticism is to become a viable and self-vindicating discipline, Wellek and Warren argued, it must be grounded in properties and concerns 'intrinsic' to its object's mode of being. As a result, theory of literature is *theoretically* made to subsume 'practical criticism' and its necessary agent, the reading subject. This shift occurs for much the same reasons, but in reverse as it were, as Richards's 'practical criticism' subsumed 'principles': to ward off the danger of critical practices turning into an anarchic and endless 'sequence of licenses' (Wimsatt 1970a, p. 27, first published 1954) for the construal of literary meaning.

Wellek's subordination of 'reading' into a conceptualized

'super-personal tradition' of works of art is part of a
larger edifice of distinctions (intrinsic/extrinsic, private/public,
diachronic/synchronic, etc.), reinforced with formalist and
structuralist theoretical concepts imported from his association
with the Prague Linguistic Circle (see Hawkes 1977, pp. 74–5).
The structure is intended to accommodate a total theory
of literature which will escape the seemingly ineluctable
quandary, inherited from Coleridge and perpetuated by
Richards, of a subject/object dichotomy.

Wellek does not share Coleridge's hesitation between the
reader and the text. 'It is true, of course', he writes, 'that a
poem can be known only through individual experiences, but
it is not identical with such an individual experience' (1949,
p. 134). The 'real' poem is not the experience of its performance
or of its author or reader, not even the collective experience of
an infinite multiplicity of readers. The work of art is a whole
and self-sufficient 'system of signs, or structure of signs,
serving a specific aesthetic purpose' (p. 129). Following the
Polish philosopher Roman Ingarden, Wellek defines the 'real'
poem as a stratified structure of implicit norms or determinations
(the sound patterns, syntactical structures, units of meaning,
etc.) realized or concretized only partially and imperfectly in
the actual experience of its many readers. This distinction
between the poem's 'virtual' (what Tate might have called
'metaphysical') existence and its various 'realizations' or
'concretizations' in the minds of its readers corresponds, he
says, to Saussure's distinction between *langue* and *parole*,
between 'the system of language and the individual speech-act'
(p. 140). Wellek postulates that 'there is no need to hypostatize
or "reify" this system of norms, to make it a sort of archetypal
idea presiding over a timeless realm of essences' (pp. 141–2),
although it is not clear how he can avoid a hypostatization
which is no less than the cornerstone of his system. Saussure's
distinction too is not without its unacknowledged problems
and hypostatizations – chiefly the arbitrary separation of
system (synchronicity) and history (diachronicity) – but these
of course serve Wellek's purposes well. They furnish him with
an extremely supple 'both/and' definition of the work of art,
which is granted both a 'timeless' fundamental structure of
identity and a dynamic dimension of historicity and change.

The literary work of art is neither an empirical fact, in the sense of being a state of mind of any given individual or of any group of individuals, nor is it an ideal changeless object such as a triangle. The work of art may become an object of experience; it is, we admit, accessible only through individual experiences, but it is not identical with any experience. It differs from ideal objects such as numbers precisely because it is only accessible through the empirical part of its structure, the sound-system, while a triangle or a number can be intuited directly. It also differs from ideal objects in one important respect. It has something which can be called 'life'. It arises at a certain point of time, changes in the course of history, and may perish.

(p. 143)

But how can a structure be said to be self-identical and also changed by history and experience? In what sense can *Beowulf* as heard by an eighth-century audience be identical with a twentieth-century reception of the work? If the poem itself, its system of norms and determinations, is available only through the recreation (which is always already an interpretation) of the sound patterns, syntactical structures, units of meaning, etc., how can we validly speak of its being a self-identical entity? The ontological question cannot be answered, on Wellek's terms, without an appeal to epistemology, for the entity referred to as the 'real' work of art is a hypostatization which, rather like the concept of the unconscious, is summoned into existence performatively. In such conditions, the distinction between ontology and ideology becomes very obscure. To call the structure 'dynamic' is either to beg the question or (more subversively than Wellek evidently intends) to problematize the concept of literary form and its supposed identity.

It has been frequently pointed out that the New Critical failure to pursue the consequences of many of its assumptions was in the interests of an aesthetic and aestheticizing ideology of literature.[2] The ontological shift undertaken by the New Criticism led to a systematic suppression of the temporality and intentionality of literary understanding. Readers are hypothetically admitted only to ensure the existence of the work of art; rather like those fleeting angels, created for the

sole purpose of a moment's magnification of their creator, they
vanish with the fulfilment of that role. I called Wellek's
formula 'supple' precisely because it contrives at once to pose
and dodge the epistemological question, or the problem of a
constituting subject.

'When doctrine totters', a fellow New Critic cautioned early
on, 'it seems it can fall only into the gulf of bewilderment; few
minds risk that fall; most seize the remnants and swear the
edifice remains, when doctrine becomes intolerable dogma'
(Blackmur 1952, p. 373). The categorical excommunication of
the reader finds its apotheosis in W.K. Wimsatt's famous
manifestos, 'The Intentional Fallacy' and 'The Affective
Fallacy' (1970a, written in collaboration with M. Beardsley,
first published 1954):

> The Intentional Fallacy is a confusion between the poem and
> its origins. . . . It begins by trying to derive the standard of
> criticism from the psychological *causes* of the poem and ends
> in biography and relativism. The Affective Fallacy is a
> confusion between the poem and its *results* (what it *is* and
> what it *does*). . . . It begins by trying to derive the standard of
> criticism from the psychological effects of the poem and ends
> in impressionism and relativism. The outcome of either
> fallacy, the Intentional or the Affective, is that the poem
> itself, as an object of specifically critical judgment, tends to
> disappear.
>
> (p. 21)

The anti-affective and anti-expressive thrust of New Criticism
could not be more explicitly spelled out. Better the disappearance of the subject than the literary object, and not even the
declarative force of Wimsatt's style can conceal the 'metaphysical pathos'. Wimsatt is perfectly candid about what is at
stake:

> The poem conceived as a thing in between the poet and the
> audience is of course an abstraction. The poem is an act.
> The only substantive entities are the poet and the audience.
> But if we are to lay hold of the poetic act to comprehend and
> evaluate it, and if it is to pass current as a critical object, it
> must be hypostatized.
>
> (p. xvii)

The New Critical legacy

'The heresy of paraphrase', 'The Intentional Fallacy', 'The Affective Fallacy' – it is in the style of doctrinaire prescriptions and rites of excommunication that we generally remember the key New Critical slogans which increasingly adopted the tones of 'defensive mastery' (Hartman 1976, p. 218). The acts of criticism they describe are aggressively proprietory; metaphors such as 'laying hold' of the poetic act, seizing and 'battering' the literary object, betray the anxious entrenchment in rigid formulae, even when, as Wimsatt shrewdly remarked in a survey of the critical scene sixteen years after the publication of *The Verbal Icon*, the question of the literary object had blurred into the question 'whether such a question can be correctly asked' ('Battering the object', 1970, p. 61).

But essential correctives both to what Hartman calls the 'New Critical reduction' (1980, p. 6) and to reductive views of the New Critical legacy can be found within their own ranks. I return therefore briefly to the margins of their discourse and to the case of one eminent New Critic who made a virtue of epistemological uncertainty. Doctrine, R.P. Blackmur reminds us, should not be taken literally, or it becomes 'omnivorous'. Doctrine is an escape from the real task of criticism which 'ought scrupulously to risk the use of any concept that seems propitious or helpful in getting over gaps. Only the use should be consciously provisional, speculative, and dramatic' (1952, first published 1935, p. 373). For the ironic critic, the chief labour of literary study should be a heuristic and sceptical engagement in 'the constant, resourceful restoration of ignorance'; he should be prepared to let go of his doctrinal crutches when, at the limit of their usefulness, they threaten to cripple the venture itself.

'A critic's job of work', the essay from which I quote, argues strongly and eloquently against 'tendencious' [sic] criticism, the kind which strives for omnipotence and represses self-awareness and the awareness of gaps. Blackmur's ironic ideal is 'technical' criticism (playing on the root meaning of *techne* – an art). We need whatever 'techniques' (tools and speculative instruments) we can muster for performing the unceasing acts of mediation we call poetry *and* criticism. But these techniques should be employed to *enact* the experience of reading – provisionally, speculatively, dramatically – not to totalize it. It is not the knowledge to be obtained or the object to be seized that concerns Blackmur, but the ways of knowing, the 'habit (not a theory) of imagination' (p. 376). That is why criticism itself ought to be a self-conscious and ironic vigilance, a 'vivid questing', which is always, from its root, a questioning. His archetypes of 'undoctrinated' thinking (Freud, Plato and Montaigne) are ironists because they always leave room for alternate ideas,

> betraying in their most intimate recesses the duplicity of every thought, pointing it out, so to speak, in the act of self-incrimination. . . . Such an approach . . . is the only rational approach to the multiplication of doctrine. . . . Anything else is a succumbing.
>
> (pp. 375–6)

And when the New Criticism succumbed to 'intolerable dogma' and retired into its tendentious critical insularity, Blackmur took it to task for bad faith, for lacking the courage of its metaphors – warning that it had betrayed its original insights into rhetoric and 'the psychology of poetic language', and was leading a false and sterile life committed to 'excess analysis, excess simplification, and excess application, which is the normal pathology of a skill become a method and a method become a methodology' (1955, pp. 190–1).

What, then, was the 'real' New Criticism? If this question can be asked at all, it is as a question of interpretation (of which New Critical writings we read, and how) rather than of history. Thumbnail sketches of New Criticism speak more of the writer's preferences and sympathies than of the object represented. Krieger has remarked that 'certain adventitious circumstances seem to be all that these critics have in common. . . . Yet [they] are commonly referred to as if they constituted a single and defined entity. This is an especially convenient device for those who want to issue a blanket condemnation of them' (1977, first published 1956, p. 4). Such condemnations continue to sprout, testifying to the extraordinary tenacity of this native tradition of criticism. Jonathan Culler's recent censures represent one view of an oppressive, anti-historicist habit of interpretation. 'The insidious legacy of the New Criticism is the widespread and unquestioning acceptance of the notion that the critic's job is to interpret literary works' (1981, p. 5); our continuing attachment to the principle of interpretation, he claims, eviscerates more urgent and better projects such as an examination of the conditions of intelligibility underlying the activity of interpretation. But bad habits are hard to relinquish: 'whatever critical affiliations we may proclaim', he adds, 'we are all New Critics, in that it requires a strenuous effort to escape notions of the autonomy of the literary work, the importance of demonstrating its unity, and *the requirement of "close reading"*' (p. 3, my emphasis). That Culler's reductive presentation of New Criticism might be an inevitable and hygienic move to clear a space for alternative criticisms is commendable, but is not my immediate concern here. What intrigues me is the presence in recent theoretically inclined Anglo-American criticism of an undue anxiety about a precursor, the shadow of whose rigid and obsolescent methodology is imagined to assume monolithic and ominous proportions.

Why should a discredited critical method continue to trouble us so persistently? Partly, no doubt (and as many have said), because the academy is reluctant to relinquish its indubitable pedagogical successes. But I should like to hazard the opinion that – in addition to the complacent inertia of institutions – contemporary Anglo-American criticism, refreshed by the bewildering influx of European ideas, is still exploring and bringing into the open the suppressed margins of its native New Critical tradition, still learning to read even more closely. Perhaps it is not the mainstream dogma that we inherit but rather the rudimentary habit of vigilant questing and questioning, a habit of reading which New Criticism implanted yet recoiled from examining or theorizing about lest the subversive dialectical interplay of theory and practice undermine the feasibility of the project.

There were, of course, the notable exceptions within the New Critical ranks.[3] Blackmur's valorization of the artful play of intelligence which the critical act releases makes him an uncanny precursor of the post-formalist self-conscious rejoicing in the inexhaustible pleasures of the text. Criticism, he says duplicitously, is 'the formal discourse of an amateur', a lover's discourse (as opposed, presumably, to a professor's – one who professes), existing on equal terms with poetic discourse as a 'criticism of life' (p. 372). Criticism cannot postulate a subservience to the 'self-evident facts' of the literary text for these, paradoxically, are the hardest to come by. Neither can it purge its own discourse of the pathos of figuration. The labour of understanding is generated by the active encounter of reader and text, of mind with mind, and mind with itself, an understanding whose status is always metaphorical, unascertainable and therefore in question.

What is it, what are they, these seeds of understanding? And if I know, are they logical? Do they take the processional form of the words I use? Or do they take a form like that of the silver backing a glass, a dark that enholds all brightness? Is every metaphor – and the assertion of understanding is our great metaphor – mixed by the necessity of its intention? What is the mixture of a word, an image, a notion?

(p. 398)

Part II

Reader-response criticisms

3
The inscribed reader: Jonathan Culler and structuralist poetics

Homo significans: such would be the new man of
structural inquiry.

(Roland Barthes, 'The structural activity')

Until the late 1950s, American critics were on the whole
preoccupied with the question of how to determine a text's
literary meaning as precisely as possible. Differences of
opinion arose as to how this might be accomplished – whether
by an appeal to stylistic and rhetorical properties, or the
conventions of genre, or the author's intention – but there was
no disagreement about the goal of determining textual
meaning. It was the subsequent recoil from New Criticism that
gave rise to a new accent on poetics, and to an actual explosion
of theoretical speculation, with structuralism at the epicentre.

In its Anglo-American adaptation literary structuralism
may be seen as the European-bred first cousin of formalism
and – more distantly – New Criticism. Text-centred and
objectivist-oriented, it assumes that the study of literature
may be founded on a progressively accumulating body of
knowledge, an aggregate of concepts, tools, taxonomies, and
procedures of discovery which enable the critic to define the
object of his study precisely and to deal with it in a 'scientific'
fashion.[1] In a slightly ironic sense, the structuralist enterprise,

which seeks to counter the thrust of New Criticism, is also the apotheosis of the New Critical dream of objectivity. This is the sense in which Northrop Frye can be seen as our proto-structuralist, 'formulating', as in the Aristotelian model, 'the broad laws of literary experience, and . . . writing as though he believed that there is a totally intelligible structure of knowledge obtainable about poetry which is not poetry itself or the experience of it, but poetics' (1966, first published 1957, p. 14).

The story of the fortunes of structuralism – its rise, and its impact upon and appropriation by American criticism – has been oft told and will not preoccupy us here.[2] My concern will be with the synoptic account which emerges from Jonathan Culler's lucid and influential exposition in *Structuralist Poetics* (1975), a book which appeared after structuralism had reached its zenith but before the full force of post-structuralist semiotics and deconstruction had registered. This particular moment furnishes the book with a vantage point precariously situated between the classical principles of structuralist thinking on the one hand and what is termed (somewhat vaguely) post-structuralist thought on the other. Since structuralism, in its classical manifestations, concentrated on the laws governing the internal construction of literary texts, and betrayed little interest either in the reader or in the content of the texts he reads, it is interesting and mildly surprising to discover that Culler's account of structuralism delineates a theory of reading – a theory repeated and elaborated in subsequent publications.

This theory is above all not a hermeneutic: it does not seek to define the rules and principles of interpretation. If structuralism exhorts us to reflect neither upon the empirical reader nor upon his interpretation but upon the conditions which govern the performance of his interpretive activities, it follows that such a reflection should lead to the adoption of a critical point of departure 'beyond' interpretation. 'In this sense structuralism effects an important reversal of perspective, granting precedence to the task of formulating a comprehensive theory of literary discourse and assigning a secondary place to the interpretation of individual texts' (Culler 1975, p. 118). When the traditional hierarchy is overturned, and the interpretation of literary texts is placed in an ancillary position, the reversal effectively divorces theory from practice, turning theory into an autonomous activity which uses the data of interpretation but has little impact on the procedures which produce the data. 'There are many tasks that confront criticism', Culler writes in a later polemical piece, 'many things we need to advance our understanding of literature, but one thing we do not need is more interpretations of literary works' (1981, p. 6). Culler's argument[3] is that the interminable procession of atomistic readings bequeathed us by New Criticism is a narrow and intellectually hollow reiteration whose naïve presupposition that 'there is a poem being read by a human being' (p. 4) is undercut by the fact that no work of art and no interpreter is free of history, society or any other system of signification.

> [The] insidious legacy of the New Criticism is the wide-spread and unquestioning acceptance of the notion that the critic's job is to interpret literary works. . . . In this critical climate it is therefore important, if only as a means of loosening the grip which interpretation has on critical consciousness, to take up a tendentious position and to maintain that, while the experience of literature may be an experience of *interpreting* works, in fact the interpretation of individual works is only tangentially related to the *understanding* of literature. To engage in the study of literature is not to produce yet another interpretation of *King Lear* but to advance one's understanding of the conventions and operations of an institution, a mode of discourse.
>
> (p. 5, my emphases)

On this view, an understanding of the conventions of interpretation is quite separate from the understanding of a literary work, and in this sense structuralism, no less than New Criticism, avoids the issue of reading, even as it addresses itself to the theory of reading.

As a fundamental premise, structuralism and semiotics treat literature as an already constituted and closed system. Viewed from a semiotic perspective, we inhabit a prison-house of signs in which our institutions, our poems and our selves are always already inscribed and interpreted. One consequence of this view is that, under the aegis of structuralism, the specificities of literary language are 'assimilated' to the structures of linguistics, and its effects are demystified by poetics. 'Criticism attuned to semiotics interprets works as semiotic explorations' (p. 37), which is to say that the object of interpretation now becomes the interpretation itself. This turn transforms semiotics into a self-regarding theoretical enterprise which, in the words of Julia Kristeva, 'turns back upon itself, [is] a perpetual self-criticism' (quoted in Culler 1981, p. 35). By a paradoxical route, the rejection of interpretation circles back to a theory not only of reading, but of the reading of reading.

This chapter, then, will be devoted to an exposition of Jonathan Culler's theory of reading. Engendered upon structuralist principles, it comes of age in a deconstructive conversion that discovers the innate impasses and impossibilities of theories of reading that privilege the subject as a source of literary meaning, or take for granted the foundational validity of something called the reading 'experience'. Without attempting an overview of structuralism, I shall begin by sketching a few of the underlying principles which shape Culler's views.

The subject of reading: Frye, Jakobson, Riffaterre

Well before Jonathan Culler or the structuralist impact on literary studies, Northrop Frye's *Anatomy of Criticism* (1957) advocated a position that may be said to have moved beyond interpretation. It is not possible to 'learn literature', Frye argued, in the sense that it is futile to discuss the experience or effect of the individual work on an individual consciousness; 'what one learns, transitively, is the criticism of literature' (p. 11), and *that* only if we conceive of criticism as 'a totally intelligible body of knowledge' (p. 16) whose laws derive from the system of literature itself. This is not the place to rehearse the anatomy of interlocking narrative categories or the system of archetypes which, in Frye's conceptualization, structure and uphold both the body of literature and the body of criticism. What is notable in the new perspective offered by this precursor of structuralism is the primary postulate: 'the assumption of total coherence' (p. 16) in the system of literature, an assumption that enables the reader to reduce all literary works to instances of the laws governing the system.

In one fundamental respect Frye's project, like that of structuralism proper, differs radically from New Criticism. By shifting the centre of interest away from the question of the inherent meaning of any given work to the more general question of the context and conditions of its knowability or readability, the archetypal critic, rather like his fellow structuralist or semiotician, shifts attention away from a mimetic or referential view of literature on to the underlying systems of coherence which govern the process of sense-making and meaning production. In other words, larger theoretical issues of the conditions or *terms of understanding* replace the narrower concern with *how to understand a particular text* espoused by 'practical criticism'. Regardless of whether these terms derive from semiotic presuppositions or Jungian archetypes, the shared assumption is that there is an autonomous system which we call literature from which derives another corresponding system which we call criticism or (more precisely, so as to distinguish it from evaluative discourse) 'poetics', and that these systems exist in a synchronic and timeless state.

Without benefit of structural linguistics, Frye had claimed that literature is an autonomous verbal structure which 'shapes itself' so that '[p]oetry can only be made out of other poems; novels out of other novels' (p. 97). Here is a key statement from *Anatomy of Criticism*:

> Literary meaning may best be described, perhaps, as hypothetical, and a hypothetical or assumed relation to the external world is part of what is usually meant by the word 'imaginative'. . . . In literature, questions of fact or truth are subordinated to *the primary literary aim of producing a structure of words for its own sake. . . . Wherever we have an autonomous verbal structure of this kind, we have literature.* Wherever this autonomous structure is lacking, we have language, words used *instrumentally* to help human consciousness do or understand something else. Literature is a specialized form of language, as language is of communication.
>
> (p. 74, my emphases)

What Frye emphasizes may be called a 'terminal' view of literary language, in opposition to an 'instrumental' view of language as a social practice, a communication. That is to say that Frye takes literary language to be a self-enclosed system in which the parts are defined in relation to each other. Such a system constitutes an end in itself without reference to readers or contexts of communication.

An essentially similar attitude to the function of literary language underlies the poetics of Roman Jakobson in whose work the confluence of Saussurean linguistics and Russian formalism serves not only to confer a new dignity on the project of poetics, but also stamps it with a distinctive linguistic complexion. Poetics, according to Jakobson, is entitled to a leading place in literary studies because it deals 'primarily with the question, *What makes a verbal message a work of art?*' and the form of this question alone is enough to suggest what Jakobson is driving at: an inquiry into the literariness of texts entails the integration of poetics into 'the global science of verbal structure' (1960, p. 350), which is linguistics.

All language, according to Jakobson, serves a communicative purpose which is realized in six functions: the referential, the emotive, the phatic, the metalingual, the conative and the poetic (see chapter 2, note 1). A focus on the message (not its content, intention or effect, but its linguistic form) produces a 'poetic' function – whence Jakobson's famous definition: 'The poetic function projects the principle of equivalence from the axis of selection into the axis of combination' (1960, p. 358). What this means is that in poetry patterns of repetition and similarity (of rhythm, sound, meaning) dominate; equivalence supplies the constitutive device of literary language. Central to these hypotheses is the attribution of a special status to literary language. Jakobson defined it as a usage which draws attention to the message rather than its referent, a function which thereby promotes the palpability of the sign and deepens the dichotomy between sign and referent. This is what he meant when he described literary language as organized violence against colloquial speech. But these formulations compromise the over-arching principle of all language serving in a communicative capacity; the subtle equivocation they introduce becomes evident when we consider Jakobson's analytic praxis.

Jakobson's exemplary readings of Shakespeare's Sonnet 129

(jointly with Lawrence G. Jones) and of Baudelaire's 'Les Chats' (jointly with Claude Lévi-Strauss) were the apogee of the formalist principle which holds that the function of poetic language consists in the maximum foregrounding of the message or utterance. These exhaustive (and occasionally exhausting) linguistic analyses are intended to lay bare the characteristically high density of recurrence (symmetry, equivalence, correspondence) occurring on the phonological, syntactic and semantic levels of patterning in poems. Part of the problem, however, is that literary language does not exist in a vacuum. Culler's shrewd critique of Jakobson (1975, pp. 55–74) has shown how astonishingly arbitrary the Jakobsonian categories of structuration and distribution can be, and how easily they can be transferred to *any* piece of language (a Jakobsonian scansion of four consecutive prose sentences of Jakobson's own discourse yields the same inventory of patterns and effectively makes the point), leaving one to wonder about the relationship of cause and effect in the creation of literary meanings. Culler draws out one implication of this when he observes that the use of linguistics as a critical tool leads to a reappraisal of the poetic function. 'No longer the key to a method of analysis, it becomes a hypothesis about the conventions of poetry as an institution and in particular about the kind of attention to language which poets and readers are allowed to assume' (p. 69). What linguistics cannot do is tell us what poems mean. 'For even in its own province the task of linguistics is not to tell us what sentences mean; it is rather to explain how they have the meanings which speakers of a language give them' (p. 74). Linguistics, in brief, is not a hermeneutic; it has little explanatory value when we come to inquire into the effects of literary language.

It is perhaps a tribute to the force of Jakobson's demonstration that the classical critique of his assumptions comes from within structuralism. In the essay entitled 'Describing poetic structures: two approaches to Baudelaire's *Les Chats*' (1966) Michael Riffaterre expounds the position that grammar is indeed 'the natural geometry of language', furnishing the analyst with ready-made tools, and thus rescuing him from the difficulty of reading. But a descriptive terminology will not read the poem for us. Riffaterre suggests that the notion that *every* linguistic structure in the poem is also a poetic one (i.e. has a poetic function or a set towards the message) is doubtful. Not all systems of correspondence need to be relevant or meaningful. He observes that in certain cases the parallelism suggested by grammar 'remains virtual because it has no homologue in the meter or in the semantic system' (p. 208); in another instance the technical meaning of 'feminine' as used in metrics is illegitimately literalized. Furthermore, some of the linguistic systems remarked by the analysts are entirely imperceptible to the 'normal' reader. Such lacunae suggest that even 'the wariest of analysts slips into a belief in the intrinsic explanatory worth of purely descriptive terms' (p. 209). The analyst should beware that linguistic categories alone will not yield the meaning or the poeticalness of literary texts.

If Jakobson's linguistic tools rebuild the literary text into a virtual 'super-poem', Riffaterre, as a counter-statement, posits the construction of a heuristic device (not a persona) named the 'super-reader'. The super-reader is like a palimpsest of available textual commentary on the poem which may include the author's statements or corrections, translations, dictionaries, etc., and 'as many critics as I could find' (p. 215). The super-reader is another system (not, however, identifiable by linguistic means), a system of intertextuality whose relevance to the understanding of the poem must be incorporated into the analysis since 'the poetic phenomenon, being linguistic, is not simply the message, but the whole act of communication' (p. 214) which encompasses not only message but also addresser and addressee. The responses recorded by the super-reader have the virtue of 'pinpoint[ing] . . . the location of the devices that trigger them' (any point in the text that gives the reader pause is tentatively considered 'a component of the poetic structure') and thus 'screening pertinent structures and only pertinent structures' (p. 215).

In a far more ambitious work entitled *The Semiotics of Poetry* (1978), Riffaterre silently abandons his super-reader in the elaboration of a total theory of poetry and of interpretation, in which the reader's activity – comparable to the activity of solving overdetermined textual puzzles – is firmly controlled and restrained by the patterns formed by poetic signs. This very control guarantees the reader's mastery of the poem. The book's argument is that the most profitable approach to the theory of poetry is semiotic. Based on the premises that the text is a finite and closed system; that meaning in poems is always indirect ('a poem says one thing and means another'); that the literary phenomenon is a dialectic between text and reader; and that a poem is a verbal construct in which meaning is achieved by reference from words to words, not to things – Riffaterre stipulates that a poem consists of variant transformations of a central invariant matrix or kernel (an 'original' word or sentence) into a text. The reader's task is to discover the invariant and originating kernel of signification.[4]

The shared impulse to methodize the reader into a function of the text and to confine his activity to a recuperative role is what emerges broadly from these representative structuralist speculations. 'Any text (and especially a literary one)', writes the semiotician Yury Lotman, 'contains in itself what we should like to term the *image of the audience* and . . . this image actively affects the real audience by becoming for it a kind of normatizing code' (1982, p. 81). From this basic insight arises a vast industry of investigations whose purpose is to produce a systematic and normative account of the reader and the reading process.[5]

From the subject of reading to the reading subject

If the poet's purpose is to make the visible a little harder to see (Wallace Stevens), structuralist accounts of the reader's role conceive of it as one of restoring literary language to meaning, rescuing it from ungrammaticality and deviance, and reintegrating it into the 'sociolect' or natural parlance of our ordinary and familiar language – in brief, mastering the poem's uncanny effects. This is the attitude to literary language that Jonathan Culler adopts when he writes that

> we are attracted to literature because it is obviously *something other than ordinary communication*; its formal and fictional qualities bespeak *a strangeness, a power*, an organiz-ation, a permanence which is foreign to ordinary speech. Yet *the urge to assimilate that power* and permanence or to let that

formal organization work upon us *requires us to make literature into a communication, to reduce its strangeness,* and to draw upon supplementary conventions which enable it, as we say, to speak to us. The difference which seemed the source of value becomes *a distance to be bridged by the activity of reading and interpretation.* The strange, the formal, the fictional, must be *recuperated or naturalized,* brought within our ken, if we do not want to remain gaping before monumental inscriptions.

(1975, p. 134, my emphases)

The motif of a bridge to provide the reader with access to meaning is probably endemic to theories of literary language. Strange, disturbing, other, devoid of a referential or instrumental function, self-sufficient and auto-referential – literary language comes to be seen as that which cannot 'speak' unless we 'recuperate' or 'naturalize' its otherwise mute and self-sufficient order of words. Thence arises the question of how to move from linguistic structures to literary meanings.

For Jakobson, as for the formalists, a theory of literature was a theory of 'literariness', a theory of the properties of a language from which certain effects can be seen to arise. Culler, by shifting the centre of interest away from the literariness of texts (i.e. from the specific differences of literary language) to the structure of readers' responses, is able to perform an adjustment which allows him to side-step the difficulties of identifying and accounting for the relationship between 'literariness' and interpretation. Poetics, in his view, makes it its business to explore the conventions and institutions which enable response. The fact that structuralism engendered a reader-response theory is thus not as anomalous or eccentric as it might at first blush appear to be. Although in its 'classical' manifestations, structuralist and semiotic analysis, as I pointed out, was not hospitable to inquiries into the reading process or the interpretive activity *per se*, its concentration on describing the processes by means of which we invest things with meaning – the rules or practices, the codes, conventions, assumptions or enabling systems of competence which make intelligibility possible – led eventually to a theory of reading. Here, in Culler's formulation, is the logic behind this move.

To account for the form and meaning of literary works is to make explicit the special conventions and procedures of interpretation that enable readers to move from the linguistic meaning of sentences to the literary meaning of works. To explain facts about the form and meaning works have for readers is to construct hypotheses about the conditions of meaning, and hypotheses about the conditions of meaning are claims about the conventions and interpretive operations applied in reading. In brief, I am arguing that if the study of literature is a discipline, it must become a poetics: a study of the conditions of meaning and thus a study of reading.

(1980, p. 49)

This is, of course, also a theory of the reader, but in the very special and circumscribed sense of a textualized reader, one who is the result rather than the cause of linguistic structures. If the styles and conventions of interpretation are a major centre of concern in structuralist poetics, a second central tenet of this mode of criticism pertains to the priority of language over subjectivity, and to the secondary or derivative status of the reading subject. 'The basis of subjectivity is in the exercise of language' (Benveniste 1971, p. 226); a subject sets himself up as a subject by referring to 'I', where 'I' can only be conceptualized in relation to a grammatical 'non-I' or 'you'. 'If one really thinks about it, one will see that there is no other objective testimony to the identity of the subject except that which he himself thus gives about himself' (p. 226). Expressed through grammatical or semiotic units, the self is a conventional construct, a function of the codes which utter it;

> once the conscious subject is deprived of its role as source of meaning – once meaning is explained in terms of conventional systems which may escape the grasp of the conscious subject – the self can no longer be identified with consciousness. It is 'dissolved' as its functions are taken up by a variety of interpersonal systems that operate through it.
> (Culler 1975, p. 28)

Semiotic criticism, therefore, eschews the notion of an individual subject engaged in disclosing the significance of an

individual text produced by an individual author. Not only is
the death of the author proclaimed by Roland Barthes; once
the author is removed, 'the claim to decipher a text becomes
quite futile' (Barthes 1977, p. 147), because the text is now
given over to the multiplicity of codes that characterize
'writing' or the interminable play of the sign. In this situation,
the destination of a text's unity and coherence is the reader
who is 'the space on which all the quotations that make up a
writing are inscribed without any of them being lost' (p. 148).
This new centre of meaning, however, is not a person or a
'subject' in the usual sense but rather a kind of generalized
knowledge or encyclopaedic language, a conglomeration of
codes which have no identifiable beginning or ending. '*I read
the text*. . . . This "I" which approaches the text is already itself
a plurality of other texts, of codes which are infinite' (Barthes
1974, p. 10), and it is in or through these codes that the subject
is constituted. 'The reader', as Culler puts it, 'becomes the
name of the place where the various codes can be located: a
virtual site' (1981, p. 38) – of intertextuality rather than
intersubjectivity. She/he/it is a textual function serving the
ends of semiotics, which are to make explicit 'the implicit
knowledge which enables signs to have meaning' (p. 38).

Literary competence

The cornerstone of Culler's theory of reading, borrowed from
linguistic parlance, is a generative notion of 'competence'. Just
as the speaker of a language has the capacity to understand
and produce an infinite number of sentences not previously
encountered, because he/she has 'internalized' a 'grammar'
and a repertoire of rules, codes and structures which enable
him/her to recognize a string of words as a meaningful
sequence – so, by analogy, the reader of literature is able to
make sense of what she/he reads because she/he has internalized
a system of rules and conventions of interpretation without
which she/he would be unable to recognize a literary text, let
alone understand it. This is the case because a literary text is
not *inherently* meaningful; it is 'an utterance that has meaning
only with respect to a system of conventions which the reader

has assimilated. If other conventions were operative its range of potential meanings would be different' (p. 116).

When we read we apply certain acquired and implicit rules or expectations about the nature of literary organization. A powerful myth of coherence compels us to make sense of gaps and indeterminacies. Such, for instance, is the rule of thematic unity (the expectation that different elements in the text will cohere within one system of signification), or the related rule of significance (the expectation that a text's figurations are not random, but will cohere in expressing a significant attitude to some issue). To the same purpose, we regularly use the orientational (deictic) features of language (e.g. personal pronouns, anaphoric articles, demonstratives) to invent strategies of construing a situation of utterance, in order to overcome the impersonal nature of poetry. Above all the reader moves to 'naturalize' – to make intelligible and 'vraisemblable' – the content of a poem by recognizing a common world of reference (whether textual or natural) which restores a communicative function to the text. 'Naturalization' is not an intuitive but a culturally determined operation of making legible and legitimate, of integrating the read into the known. 'To assimilate or interpret something is to bring it within the modes of order which culture makes available, and this is usually done by talking about it in a mode of discourse which culture takes as natural. This process goes by various names in structuralist writing: recuperation, naturalization, motivation, *vraisemblablisation*' (p. 137). All these are modes and procedures of bringing the strange or deviant into an acceptable discursive order. Such rules are 'the constituents of the institution of literature' (p. 116), the codes of a *langue*, as the structuralists would say, with respect to which individual instances of *parole* acquire meaning. The sum total of these codes makes up an internalized knowledge or competence, a 'mastery' that enables an author to produce a text and a reader to understand it. The task of poetics is not to prescribe these codes or to postulate norms for correct reading, but rather to disclose and make explicit their implicit force.

From a perspective which views understanding as a universally established, rule-governed process, the object of interest cannot be an individual reading, but the general conventionality of reading. A good portion of *Structuralist Poetics* is devoted to an account of this conventionality. To speak of the meaning of a work is not to elaborate the inherent properties or senses of the text, but to give an account of what happens to the reader, or what the reader does. What happens, in Culler's view, is the exercise of a reader's literary competence, the bringing to bear of a whole latent system of interpretive conventions for deciphering the meaning of literary texts. The obvious implication is that the literary meaning which these operations elicit does not refer to individual experience. 'The meaning of a poem within the institution of literature is not, one might say, the immediate and spontaneous reaction of individual readers but the meanings which they are willing to accept as both plausible and justifiable when they are explained' (p. 124). The question is not what an individual reader might do, but what the 'ideal' reader does. And what the ideal reader does is to 'naturalize' the text.

On these principles, as Culler admits, anything can be made to signify; anything can be brought 'into relations with a type of discourse or model which is already, in some sense, natural and legible' (p. 138), whether by making the text correspond to something in the world, or to something in another text. Even the absurd, the chaotic or the incoherent can be allegorized into a statement about the absurd, the chaotic or the incoherent. 'Any work can be made intelligible if one invents appropriate conventions. . . . If a difficult work later becomes intelligible it is because new ways of reading have been developed in order to meet what is the fundamental demand of the system: the demand for sense' (p. 123). The import of this argument is that some interpretation is always guaranteed and that consequently there would be no aberrant texts, just as there are no aberrant readings; in effect, to interpret becomes an act of obliterating the difference or otherness of literature, domesticating or coercing into 'natural- ness' the strangeness which defies and resists understanding. From Culler's point of view, this is precisely the enabling assumption of poetics: every interpretation is an instance of the laws governing the system of interpretation.

Culler is not unaware that all this implies an idealizing

impulse, but the presupposition is not always acknowledged and leads to a certain ambivalence. In the case of the concept of an 'ideal' reader (the official portrait, evidently, of the professional critic), Culler was careful to clear up the ambivalence. His initial position that '[t]he ideal reader is, of course, a theoretical construct, perhaps best thought of as a representation of the central notion of acceptability' (p. 124) gave way to the recognition that the term 'ideal' is infelicitous in its suggestion of the existence of an ideal reading. In a subsequent reformulation, Culler got rid of the residue of metaphysical pathos, noting that the construction of reading models, as models, will have to be idealizations, 'but notions of an ideal reader or a super-reader ought to be avoided. To speak of an ideal reader is to forget that reading has a history' (1981, p. 51). This is an important revision that enables Culler to appeal to the practice of actual readers for evidence of facts about reading.

The concept of 'facts', however, is too easily taken for granted. To explain 'facts' about literary works, about their form and meaning, is, Culler claims, to specify the conditions or systems of intelligibility which govern reading. But what is a *fact* if not, by a circular route, the product of these systems? In his account, some 'essential' facts would be: that reading poetry is a rule-governed process; that there is a range of agreement or disagreement about a certain text, or that a work can have a variety of meanings, but not just any meaning; that certain meanings become canonical; or that works which seem unintelligible do nevertheless get explained. It appears that 'facts' are carefully selected instances of consensual critical practice. The question, however, arises (and it is one to which Stanley Fish addresses himself) whether facts are indeed 'essential' in the sense of universal, absolute and transhistorical, or whether they are themselves the product of a system of agreement about what will count as a 'fact'. Even the view that the reading of poetry is a rule-governed process is not a 'fact' in any essentialist sense. It is not accidental that Culler's presuppositions regarding facts are not permitted to interrogate the status of his own discourse, since the project of a theory of reading seeks to found itself on a certain notion of facts.

Even more disconcerting is the doubleness which governs

the central concept of 'mastery' on which the notion of literary competence hinges. The meaning of the phrase 'mastery of the system' is disrupted by an ambiguous genitive, so that the question arises whether it is the reader who is master of the systems of intelligibility or whether he is himself over-mastered by the systems. This equivocation informs Culler's account of literary competence which subscribes on the one hand to the semiotic axiom of the dissolution of the subject, but which concludes, on the other, with a rousing variation on the humanist theme of 'know thyself':

> An awareness of the assumptions on which one proceeds, an ability to make explicit what one is attempting to do, makes it easier to see where and how the text resists one's attempts to make sense of it and how, by its refusal to comply with one's expectations, it leads to that questioning of the self and of ordinary social modes of understanding which has always been the result of the greatest literature. . . . How better to facilitate a reading of oneself than by trying to make explicit one's sense of the comprehensible and the incomprehensible . . . literature challenges the limits we set to the self as a device of order and allows us, painfully or joyfully, to accede to an expansion of self.
>
> (1975, pp. 129–30)

In an astonishingly unsemiotic spirit, the entire thrust towards normativization inscribed in Culler's poetics of reading is here overturned by an incipient reversal and deconstruction of his position. Reading *against* the grain or against received opinion leads to a volte-face, as a consequence of which it ceases to be clear that interpretation is subordinated to poetics, or that the positions of master and slave (who controls what) are stable; literature now reappears in the role of the antagonistic other of poetics: that which resists and defies assimilation and naturalization.

And so, finally, structuralism's reversal of perspective can lead to a mode of interpretation based on poetics itself, where the work is *read against* the conventions of discourse and where one's interpretation is an account of the ways in which the work complies with or *undermines* our procedures for making sense of things. Though it does not, of course, replace ordinary thematic interpretations, *it does avoid premature foreclosure – the unseemly rush from word to world – and stays within the literary system for as long as possible*. . . . In this kind of interpretation the meaning of the work is what it shows the reader, by the acrobatics in which it involves him, about the problems of his condition as *homo significans*, maker and reader of signs.

(p. 130, my emphases)

It may safely be said that this is the discourse of a deconstructed structuralist[6] hovering indecisively between an affirmation of (self)-knowledge and its denial, between asserting the canny control a reader has over his text, and admitting the text's uncanny evasions of this control. It would be simplistic, as well as not quite accurate, to say that Culler's text suffers from incoherence; that *homo significans* has bent or misread the signs of his readerhood.[7] Rather, it seems to me that Culler's discourse here eloquently, albeit blindly, voices its own limits, manifesting (to repeat a metaphor that has become a cliché of contemporary discourse) the blind spot in a vision on the edge of discovering its limitations but recoiling from the discovery. The discovery is that reading is not by any means a 'mastery'.

The deconstructive swerve

'Deconstruction explores the problematic situation to which stories of reading have led us. If it can be seen as the culmination of recent work on reading, it is because projects which began with something quite different in mind are brought up against the questions that deconstruction addresses' (Culler 1982, p. 83) – questions that have to do with the (im)possibility of reading itself. This is the informing orientation of *On Deconstruction: Theory and Criticism after Structuralism* (1982), Jonathan Culler's 'sequel' to *Structuralist Poetics*.

Despite its different premises, methods and conclusions the book may be seen as an authentic sequel in two senses. In the first place it reopens to scrutiny the confident synthesis of *Structuralist Poetics* according to which 'man is not just *homo sapiens* but *homo significans*: a creature who gives sense to things'

(1975, p. 264). If in 'the final analysis' we are nothing other than the products of our system of reading and writing, then we should aspire to control the means of production, for 'he who does not actively take up and work upon this system – is himself "written" by the system. He becomes the product of a culture which eludes him' (p. 264). This confident foreclosure is marginally but pointedly qualified in the book's concluding sentence which asserts that 'as yet we understand very little about how we read' (p. 265), a sentence that serves to put in question all the enabling strategies and competences by which we supposedly master what we read in order to 'give sense to things'. In taking on the task of mediating the strategies of a rival and antithetical programme of reading and writing, Culler undertakes a course that will test the courage of his convictions precisely because the validity of his earlier project is jeopardized by such a test.

But *On Deconstruction* is a sequel in another less hazardous sense – the sense in which, 'when so many of yesterday's structuralists are today's post-structuralists' (1982, p. 25), post-structuralism may fairly be viewed as the natural or logical consequence of structuralism. Culler rejects the sometimes ignorant and frequently crude distinctions between two discontinuous modes or phases, the earlier of which is canny and rational, the later uncanny and alogical, one a quest for knowledge with its own rules, the other an unbridled questioning of all knowledge.[8] Deconstruction, in his view, is not the simple undoing of structuralist delusions but is an even closer kind of reading, the kind which teases out further twists or discriminations inscribed in the texts of structuralism. 'Observers often assume that if post-structuralism has succeeded structuralism it must have refuted it, or at least transcended it: *post hoc ergo ultra hoc* . . . but the opposition between the *canny* and the *uncanny* resists it, for the uncanny is neither a refutation of nor a replacement for the canny' (p. 24). It is, as Freud taught us, the *return* of the repressed, the reenactment of a familiar but 'forgotten' or displaced drama.

With respect to the concerns of a reader-response criticism, the play of displacements revolves around the distribution of labour between the text and the reader. Culler addresses himself specifically to the metacritical question of why reader-response theories have been unable to account satisfactorily for how much control is exercised by the reader and how much by the text, a difficulty that affects the stabilization of the text–reader relationship. 'To read is to operate with the hypothesis of a reader' (p. 67), but what is at stake, Culler asks, in the appeal to a reader's 'experience' as the grounding term of a theory of reading? How is the status of the text affected? How is the dialectic of reading structured? Above all, 'what sort of system prevents the working out of a noncontradictory synthesis?' (p. 82)

Briefly put, the answer is 'difference and division'. Culler's critique of reader-response theories focuses on the misguided appeal to anything we might wish to call natural or immediate in response; what reader-response theories reveal is the heavily mediated and divided nature of response. The appeal to what readers 'do' is an appeal to an extremely problematic category because it can never be immediately accessible. What is accessible instead is a *narrative* of what readers do. 'To speak of the meaning of a work is to tell a story of reading' (p. 35) rather than to report an incontrovertible fact. The foundational term 'experience' takes for granted the unity and identity (or, if you like, the presence) of the reading subject to himself, but what is actually described is neither present nor immediate; it is a hypothesis, an invented construct, for 'experience', as Culler puts it, 'is divided and deferred – already behind us as something to be recovered, yet still before us as something to be produced. The result is not a new foundation but stories of reading' (p. 82). In effect, theories of reading describe experience by staging *representations* of reading, creating narratives of experience in which the reader is assigned a role. 'To read is to play the role of a reader and to interpret is to posit an experience of reading . . . it is to imagine what "a reader" would feel and understand. To read is to operate with the hypothesis of a reader, and there is always a gap or division within reading' (p. 67), a distance or separation between what happens, and the staged report of what happens. This gap gives rise to an inevitable structure of oscillation in the stories of reading.

Theories of reading stories and descriptions of reading

stories seem themselves to be governed by aspects of story. But there is another structural necessity at work in the switches back and forth between the reader's dominance and the text's dominance. A study of reading would not permit one to decide between these alternatives, for the situation can be theorized from either perspective, and there are reasons why it must be theorized from both perspectives. . . . No compromise formulation, with the reader partly in control and the text partly in control, would accurately describe this situation, which is captured, rather, by juxtaposition of two absolute perspectives. The shift back and forth in stories of reading between readers' decisive actions and readers' automatic responses is not a mistake that could be corrected but an essential structural feature of the situation.

(p. 73)

This structure leads Culler to the conclusion that reader-response criticisms desire to postulate a monism of theory which finds itself struggling with and subverted by the dualism of narrative, and no compromise formulation can capture the essentially divided quality of reading. 'Theories of reading demonstrate the impossibility of establishing well-grounded distinctions between fact and interpretation, between what can be read in the text and what is read into it. . . . There must always be dualisms: an interpreter and something to interpret, a subject and an object, an actor and something he acts upon or that acts on him' (p. 75).

For the taxonomically-minded Culler (who is nothing if not canny), the reader's fortunes in contemporary criticism can now be represented by means of two kinds of plot. In one, the reader would be the hero, successfully overcoming textual obstacles in the achievement of his quest for meaning and for self-realization. The stories told by Michael Riffaterre, Norman Holland and Wolfgang Iser – indeed, by all so-called reader-response criticisms – belong to this category of narratives with a happy ending. The onset of deconstruction, however, has generated an alternative plot in which the reader is the agonist or anti-hero, manipulated by an uncanny text which puts in question his ill-starred quest for meaning. The denouement of this latter plot leads to frustration, misreading, and gothic power struggles. The critics whose narratives belong in this category (J. Hillis Miller, for example, or Paul de Man) do not consider themselves reader-response critics, and some (like Harold Bloom) are more than eager to be dissociated from deconstruction. Nevertheless, their post-structuralist modes of criticism will likewise find themselves telling some story of reading.

Culler too tells a story – the story of a story. His adoption of the model of narration is a transcending metacritical move which has its own narrative allure or decorum. It aspires to the structure, we might say, of a monistic narrative, the story to end stories, by writing the ultimate denouement (or obituary) of the reader-response project: exhausted by the irresolvable and irreducible struggles for authority between textual constraint and reader's experience, reader-response criticism leaves the stage free for reading on an ongoing transferential model shaped by the structural necessity of analysis terminable and interminable. However, we shall here suspend the question whether such a story can have a sequel or an ending, in order to turn to some of these other narratives of reading.

4
Literature in the reader: Stanley Fish and affective poetics

The truest respect which you can pay to the reader's understanding, is to halve this matter amicably, and leave him something to imagine, in his turn. . . . For my own part, I am eternally paying him compliments of this kind, and do all that lies in my power to keep his imagination as busy as my own.

(Laurence Sterne, *Tristram Shandy*)

The Reader's first major appearance[1] on the stage of English studies took place in the heyday of structuralism, when she/he premiered in no less auspicious a setting than Paradise. In *Surprised by Sin: The Reader in Paradise Lost* (1967) Stanley Fish argued that 'the poem's centre of reference is its reader who is also its subject', and that Milton's purpose is to educate the reader by steering him to an awareness of his plight as fallen man, and to a sense of 'the distance which separates him from the innocence once his' (p. 1). In this view, the narrative strategy of *Paradise Lost* establishes a parallel between the situation in Paradise and the reader's situation, forcing the reader to revaluate his/her own relationship to the legitimate uses of rational and analytic inquiry on the one hand and faith on the other. 'The freedom of the Fall (and therefore man's responsibility for it) is a point of doctrine, and the reader must resist the temptation to submit it to the scrutiny of reason, just as Adam and Eve must maintain the irrelevancy of reason to the one easy prohibition' (p. 244). By recreating the drama of the Fall in the mind of the reader, the various rhetorical strategies of *Paradise Lost* prompt him/her to experience the struggle between faith and reason and consequently to see the Fall with the same 'troubled clarity' with which Adam sees. The reader is thus impelled to play the double role of active participant in the events as well as critic of his/her own performance.

As Fish put it retrospectively: 'Milton's strategy in the poem is to make the reader self-conscious about his own responses and to bring him to the realization that his inability to read the poem with any confidence in his own perception is its focus. In 1967 this was a daring argument' (1980, p. 21) because in centring the reader as the protagonist of *Paradise Lost* Fish appeared to court the Affective Fallacy. But in point of fact, the principles underlying his critical procedure are still quite orthodox, faithful to a traditional, text-centred method of 'close reading' that lapses into neither the Intentional nor Affective Fallacies. The role of the reader and the author's intention are both extrapolated from the text which – in line with Wimsatt's stern precepts – at once controls the reader's experience and reveals Milton's purposes.

Nevertheless, the novelty of the thematic shift of emphasis within what is still a 'practical' criticism – the shift which finds the reader's experience of exegetical perplexity inscribed in the text – was the harbinger of Fish's subsequent attempts to give a theoretical account of the double plot of understanding in which reader and text are enmeshed. Fish's vigorous and consistently polemical output following *Surprised by Sin* reveals a characteristic, progressively self-revising structure of concerns. Beginning with a swerve away from the orthodox New Critical view of the reader as extrinsic to the text, it moves towards an inquiry into the complications and complicities of the reader inscribed in and produced by the text, then to a revisionary relocation of textual meaning in the reader's 'experience', and finally to an escape from the text/reader dichotomy in the monistic concept of 'interpretive communities' – the concept which designates the always already given systems and institutions of interpretive authority that engender both readers and texts.

The reader's share

Perhaps the essay most directly responsible for enfranchising the critical orientation that came to be identified as 'reader-response' criticism is Fish's 'Literature in the reader: affective stylistics' (1970). Its argument takes off from the structuralist postulate of binary oppositions – subject/object, reader/text, description/interpretation, spatial/temporal, intrinsic/extrinsic – a matrix on which the structure of reversal, exclusion and supplementarity invited by theorizations of the reading act is articulated. (The attempts to escape this matrix, as we shall see, give shape to Fish's subsequent revisions of his model, leading to the demise of the affective stylistics programme.)

The argument of the essay comes into being against Wimsatt and Beardsley's despotic expulsion of the reader; the outcome of the Affective Fallacy, they had claimed, 'is that the poem itself as an object of specifically critical judgement tends to disappear' (1954, p. 2). It is precisely this disappearance that Fish embraces as the cornerstone of his affective stylistics. His own thesis is boldly articulated in either/or dualistic terms: to view a text (utterance, sentence, poetic line, stanza) as a thing-in-itself is to 'spatialize' and formalize what is essentially an ephemeral and temporal experience; it is to claim objectivity and autonomy for what is subjective and contingent. Meaning does not reside in the text because, as Fish sees it,

> [t]he objectivity of the text is an illusion and, moreover, a dangerous illusion, because it is so physically convincing. The illusion is one of self-sufficiency and completeness. A line of print or a page or a book is so obviously *there* – it can be handled, photographed, or put away – that it seems to be the sole repository of whatever value and meaning we associate with it. (I wish the pronoun could be avoided, but in a way *it* makes my point.) This is of course the unspoken assumption behind the word 'content.' The line or page or book *contains* – everything.
>
> (1970, p. 140)

Fish proposes to relocate meaning in the reader by replacing the illusory objectivity of the text with the 'experience' of a reading subject. A sentence, he claims, is an *event*, 'something that *happens* to, and with the participation of the reader. And it is this event, this happening – all of it and not anything that could be said about it or any information one might take away from it – that is, I would argue, the *meaning* of the sentence' (p. 125). If our operational question is 'what does this sentence do?' instead of 'what does this sentence mean?' then the properly temporal nature of the mental drama of understanding will assert itself, and interpretation will become '*an analysis of the developing response of the reader in relation to the words as they succeed one another in time*' (pp. 126–7); it will examine the drama of cognitive mediation taking place in the encounter of text and mind.

One of Fish's examples is a line from *Paradise Lost* (I, 335); 'Nor did they not perceive the evil plight', is an utterance which, as he provocatively puts it, '(conveniently) says nothing'. This is how the analysis proceeds:

> The first word of this line . . . generates a rather precise (if abstract) expectation of what will follow: a negative assertion which will require for its completion a subject and a verb. There are then two 'dummy' slots in the reader's mind waiting to be filled. This expectation is strengthened . . . by the auxiliary 'did' and the pronoun 'they.' Presumably, the verb is not far behind. But in its place the reader is presented with a second negative, one that cannot be accommodated within his projection of the utterance's form. His progress through the line is halted and he is forced to come to terms with the intrusive (because unexpected) 'not.' In effect what the reader *does*, or is forced to do, at this point, is ask a question – did they or did they not? – and in search of an answer he either rereads, in which case he simply repeats the sequence of mental operations, or goes forward, in which case he finds the anticipated verb, but in either case the syntactical uncertainty remains unresolved. . . .
>
> To clean the line up [by invoking, e.g., the rule of the double negative] is to take from it its most prominent and important effect – the suspension of the reader between the alternatives its syntax momentarily offers. What is a

> problem if the line is considered as an object, a thing-in-itself, becomes a *fact* when it is regarded as an occurrence.
>
> (pp. 125–6)

The insistence on the exegetical drama of construing the sense is of course not particularly original. It will be recalled that the metaphor of reading as a dramatic (and, by extension, temporal) event was central in the discourse of virtually all New Critics. But their avoidance of the reading subject confined the drama to an exclusively formal arena and thus contrived to suppress the difference between the text and its temporal realization in a reading consciousness, permitting them to fix or, as Fish has it, 'spatialize' the event and to resolve the drama into a unitary form in which the text and its completed reading coincide. This 'forgetful' bracketing of the temporal factor is precisely the tell-tale omission or suppression which reminds us, as Paul de Man has pointed out, that

> form is never anything but a process on its way to completion. . . . It is constituted in the mind of the interpreter as the work discloses itself in response to his questioning. But this dialogue between work and interpreter is endless. The hermeneutic understanding is always by its very nature lagging behind.
>
> (1983, pp. 31–2)

Fish's emphasis on the temporality of understanding would seem to imply a move to establish the theory of reading on this lag or gap. What he initially undertakes, however, is a reversal of the hierarchy of binary oppositions (text/reader, object/subject, spatial/temporal, etc.) in order to exclude the term (text, object, spatial) valorized by the formalists. But the reversal alone does not liberate Fish from the spatializing premises of the formalist system he sets out to challenge. To assume that the 'experience' of reading coincides with interpretation is to ignore or suppress anew the difference or lag of understanding. That this is indeed a suppression is indicated by Fish's marginalized admission to the division which haunts his category of 'experience' as a unit of analysis: 'The meaning of an utterance . . .', he cautions towards the end of his essay, 'is its experience – all of it – and that experience is immediately compromised the moment you say anything about it. It follows, then, that we shouldn't try to analyze language at all. The human mind, however, seems unable to resist the impulse to investigate its own processes' (1970, p. 160). In other words, no discursive *analysis* of the event of reading will coincide with the reading *experience* which, if it is to be itself, must remain private, mute, inexpressible. But since this gap between experience and its representations would devalue, if not altogether terminate, the reader-response mode of analysis before it has begun, it must be suppressed.

Fish's suppression of the difference between experience and talk about it may be illustrated by considering the way in which the concept of 'event', used to restore the temporal dimension of reading, contains within itself (and therefore fails to abrogate) the antithesis of temporal and spatial. Both etymologically and in common usage, the word 'event' signifies both the occurrence or happening (an open or 'temporal' category), as well as its fixed outcome or result (a spatial category). The centring concept of 'event' used to invoke the category of a process uncannily constrains Fish to draw upon its excluded opposite (a result), which continues to be a constitutive condition of the 'experience' of reading as he describes it.

If the description of the experience or event of reading does not (can never) coincide with the experience itself, what it can, nonetheless, do is postulate a heuristic construct or hypothesis of the *role* it would be appropriate for the reader to play. But this role, as Jonathan Culler has shown, is determined not by 'experience' but by the inevitable 'gap or division' within reading. From this it follows that 'what Fish reports is not Stanley Fish reading but Stanley Fish imagining reading as a Fishian reader . . . his accounts of the reading experience are reports of Fish reading as a Fishian reader reading as a Fishian reader' (Culler 1982, pp. 66, 67). In other words, what Fish actually describes is not a *fact* about reading or a *strategy* of reading, but a structure of the regressive deferral of reading.

Fish's depiction of the 'informed reader' also suffers from division or self-difference. Conceptualized as a competent speaker of the language, who possesses 'the semantic knowledge that a mature . . . listener brings to his task of comprehension', as well as 'literary competence' – the internalized knowledge of the properties of literary discourse (1970, pp. 144–5) – the informed reader proves to be no particular individual but, like Riffaterre's super-reader, is a linguistic and cultural ideal, a construct wavering between the empirical and the theoretical – 'neither an abstraction, nor an actual living reader, but a hybrid – a real reader (me) who does everything within his power to make himself informed' (p. 145). He is a creature whose uncertain 'self' is systematically cancelled out by a textual structure of constraints, his every operation determined by the systems of linguistic and literary competence to which he is subject. As Fish himself later came to see, the informed reader is 'an extension of formalist principles, as his every operation is said to be strictly controlled by the features of the text' (1980, p. 7). Wimsatt and Beardsley would no doubt have welcomed such a hypostatized instrument of reading. But from an affective perspective, the informed reader cuts a sorry figure as Fish's critics were quick to point out.[2] Not only does he generate an undignified sequence of false surmises and untenable hypotheses as he moves from error to error, always surprised yet curiously never learning to anticipate surprise, but, in his pursuit of the propositional truths which the text regularly denies him, he is also entirely subject to the authority of textual constraints. Fish's denial of the text's objectivity and his privileging of the reader's activity *appears* to grant the reader authority for the production of textual meaning, but it quickly transpires that this authority is even more illusory than the text's objectivity because in order for the 'event' of meaning production to occur, Fish must assume that the 'illusory' textual object is also somehow a stable and objective pattern in relation to which the event of reading occurs.

In short, this theoretical return of the reader is founded on two mutually exclusive and contradictory claims. On the one hand the theory posits a reader whose mind is the conscious, competent and responsible agent of meaning production, but on the other it proclaims him to be the product of a determinate and pre-existing structure of norms. Controlled by the systems of competence he has internalized, the reader can produce only those meanings (or bewilderments) he is programmed (by his competence or by the author of his text) to produce. This doubleness circles back to the question of the authority underwriting literary meanings, and to yet another version of the recoil from the impasse of reading.

The dialectical text

The plot thickened considerably with the publication of Fish's next book, *Self-Consuming Artifacts: The Experience of Seventeenth-Century Literature* (1972), in which the conflict between reader and text remains essentially unresolved. The thesis that 'the proper object of analysis is not the work but the reader' (p. 4) is restated, but in effect remains subordinated to, and indeed somewhat at odds with, the book's central historical and stylistic orientation. Although Fish extends his new reading practice to various forms of seventeenth-century literature (Herbert's poetry, Bacon's essays, *The Pilgrim's Progress*, the prose of Sir Thomas Browne, Milton's *The Reason of Church Government*, Burton's *Anatomy of Melancholy*), the protagonist this time is on the whole the text – a text whose disruptive and discontinuous features serve, in John Donne's words, 'to trouble the understanding, to displace, and to discompose, and disorder the judgement' (quoted in Fish 1972, p. 380).

The introductory chapter of *Self-Consuming Artifacts* outlines a stylistic frame of reference by positing two modes of literary representation which Fish (following Plato) identifies as the 'rhetorical' and the 'dialectical'. This traditional opposition is appropriated by Fish to rename the stylistic polarity variously designated by literary historians of the seventeenth century as Anglican-Puritan, or Painted-Plain, or Ciceronian-Senecan. Each style, Fish argues, betokens a different world view, and the triumph of one style over the other by the end of the century points to an important epistemological shift which cuts across religious, ideological and political affiliations. Fish's canny renaming of the opposition has the virtue of at once foregrounding certain peculiarities of style and theme and simultaneously intertwining the historical argument with a stylistic distinction between different strategies of representation, which, in turn, implicate the reader differently in the reception of the text. At first blush it looks as though literary history, formalism and affective stylistics can be happily wedded. But the duplicities of the epistemology of representation put in doubt the precision of Fish's distinction between 'rhetoric' and 'dialectic', and, by extension, his prescriptive view of the reader's role.

The distinction between 'rhetorical' and 'dialectical' texts is not unlike the distinction Roland Barthes outlines in *S/Z* between the 'readerly' and the 'writerly' text.[3] For Fish a 'rhetorical' representation refers to a mode which satisfies the needs and expectations of its readers; it mirrors for them, and presents for their approval, the opinions they already hold. Such a mode is both flattering and reassuring; it appeases and pacifies the reader by proceeding along familiar discursive and rational paths to a point of certainty and clarity. In opposition to this self-satisfying style of representation, the 'dialectical' mode unsettles, disturbs and 'de-certainizes' our expectations.

> A dialectical presentation . . . is disturbing, for it requires of its readers a searching and rigorous scrutiny of everything they believe in and live by. It is didactic in a special sense; it does not preach the truth, but asks its readers to discover the truth for themselves, and this discovery is often made at the expense not only of a reader's opinions and values, but of his self-esteem.
>
> (pp. 1–2)

A 'dialectical' text, instead of reflecting the disposition of things in a knowable, phenomenal world, brings into view the reader's consciousness, his experience of epistemological perplexity. The purpose of its style is not to affirm the received and approved, but to induce an experience of deliberate intellectual uncertainty in the reader, urging and instructing him towards a self-denying visionary aquiescence or 'conversion' beyond language. In this sense the dialectical text is not an end in itself – a transparent message – but rather the means of inducing and foregrounding the work of interpretation and understanding; the text both sets in motion and throws into relief the consciousness of reading, the laborious business of construing, surmising, articulating, hypothesizing and hypostatizing an elusive referential meaning. The meaning of the dialectical text is not to be found in any clear (or oblique) reference to some available system of knowledge, but in the mental event of hesitation and bewilderment whose outcome Fish describes as the 'conversion'.

A sentence such as Augustine's 'Illuc ergo venit ubi erat' (He came to a place where he was already) is paradigmatic of the characteristic effects a 'dialectical' text will reproduce on a large scale.

> [T]he forward (linear) movement of the syntax is countered by the feeling a reader has at the end of the sentence that he has returned to its beginning. Augustine, in effect, has made language defeat itself by making it point away from the temporal–spatial vision it naturally reflects . . . what [the language] does is alert the reader to its inability (which is also his inability) to contain, deal with, capture, say anything about its putative subject, Christ. The sentence is thus a ploy in the strategy of conversion, impressing upon the reader or hearer, the insufficiency of one way of seeing in the hope that he will come to replace it with something better.
>
> (pp. 41–2)

Such a sentence is 'the vehicle of its own abandonment', a self-consuming artefact which, phoenix-like, 'succeeds at its own expense' (p. 3). Its propositional failure is its triumph as a mental event, for it unsettles the reader's cognitive expectations by shifting from a 'rhetorical', discursive and rational mode of proposition to a 'dialectical', anti-discursive and anti-rational mode of illumination: 'the moment of its full emergence', Fish says, 'is marked by the transformation of the visible and segmented world into an emblem of its creator's indwelling presence ("thy word is all, if we could spell" (George Herbert, "The Flower")), and at that moment the motion of the rational consciousness is stilled, for it has become indistinguishable from the subject of its inquiry' (pp. 41–2).

If we suppose, for the sake of argument, that the style in which Fish writes aspires to be 'rhetorical' – i.e. a style which proceeds along discursive and rational paths to a point of referential certainty and clarity – then something odd comes into view. We might note in the sentence I have just quoted a mimicry of the self-consuming process it describes, and therefore a micro-instance of how tenuous the distinction

between 'rhetorical' and 'dialectical' can be. The thrust of the
syntax in Fish's sentence hinges on the rapid transformations
of the referential 'it'; the initial possessive pronominal adjective
'its', in the context of the paragraph, refers to the dialectical
mode, but 'it' succeeds in rapidly blurring its clear deictic
function with the effect of eventually collapsing 'rational
consciousness' into the 'subject of inquiry' (in itself a phrase
of indeterminate reference: language? the reality beyond
language? the perceiving self?).[4] My carping commentary is
not intended to fault what may be a minor stylistic fluke or
obscurity in the critic's style but to draw attention to the larger
issue of the conflict of understanding that may attend all
reading. Fish's basic insight, that reading is a problem, that it
is a narrative of the temporal and dialectical process of
understanding – and not its reduction to a statement or
conclusion – is haunted by its subversive other: the desire for
'rhetorical' propositional truths. This doubleness puts in
question the propositional authority of Fish's own theoretical
discourse.

The question manifests itself in a variety of ways in Fish's
discourse. Consider for instance the heightened moral (indeed,
evangelical) tone of the book's expository chapter, entitled
'The aesthetic of the good physician', whose rhetoric seems to
take colour from the content of the texts Fish analyses. In his
high claim, that the cathartic or therapeutic value of the
dialectical text derives from its homeopathic ability to convey
us beyond uncertainty to a world where 'the lines of
demarcation between places and things fade in the light of an
all-embracing unity' (p. 3), Fish offers with one 'rhetorical' or
teleological hand (the totalizing moment of illumination, the
stilling of the ratiocinative consciousness in a singular,
transcendent 'conversion' experience which outlasts the duration
of reading) what he snatches away with his other 'dialectical'
hand (the temporality of the reading experience, the perpetual
motion of the reader's cognitive uncertainty). Not only does
this double gesture put in doubt the usefulness or stability of
the rhetorical/dialectical set of oppositions; uncannily it mimes
the features of the texts on which Fish comments, betraying
thereby the inability of commentary to situate itself beyond or
outside its object. It is as though commentary can only repeat

and replay, in an act of unconscious complicity, the text's deferred plenitude of affirmations or denials, of which the reader is a shadow or phantom creation.

The thesis of *Self-Consuming Artifacts* at large remains haunted by an uncertainty about who or what is self-consumed – text? speaker's self? interpreter's self? commentary? Given this uncertainty, there is no logical reason why *our* experience of reading Fish's text should be any different from *his* experience of reading, say, the *Phaedrus* in which he finds 'two plots; Socrates and Phaedrus are busily building up a picture of the ideal orator while the reader is extracting, from the same words and phrases, a radical criticism of the ideal'. Reading, just like the text, can adopt two alternative styles; in one we read with the text, in the other, against it. If the counterplot of reading has the effect of undoing the text's rhetorical edifice, then to read *Self-Consuming Artifacts* is, as Fish says of the *Phaedrus*, to use it up, to see it as a 'self-consuming artifact',

> a mimetic enactment in the reader's experience of the platonic ladder in which each rung, as it is negotiated, is kicked away. The final rung, the level of insight that stands (or, more properly, on which the reader stands) because it is the last, is, of course, the rejection of written artifacts, a rejection that, far from contradicting what has preceded, corresponds exactly to what the reader, in his repeated abandoning of successive stages in the argument, has been doing.
>
> (p. 13)

The evident upshot of this *p(h)antomime* of reading is that the reader, having discarded or used up the text, has *nothing* but his own consciousness of uncertainty to stand on. Unless we find ourselves able to read the 'conversion' metaphor in its strictly religious sense (and most of us don't in fact convert upon reading seventeenth-century texts), a 'conversion' experience must represent an allegory of the reader's unavoidable, infinitizing repetition of the text's strategy which has cunningly led him up the steep Hill of Cognition at whose vertiginous summit it abandons him suspended – beyond time, place or language – over the Abyss of Unknowability. But the implication that criticism too must disappear into this 'dumbfoundering abyss/Between us and the object' (Wallace Stevens, 'St John and the Back-Ache') is an allegory controverted by the counter-allegory of a critical text whose argument – that visionary transcendence rejects language – must necessarily retain language to authorize its precarious propositions. What remains, therefore, is an undeniably ghostly residue of wandering signifiers.

It is only fair to add that the (im)possible (in)coherence of Fish's undertaking, which – on its own self-declared terms – cannot survive its own performance, is only indirectly the salient issue in this story. It is because Fish proffers an abundance of accomplished interpretations which succeed brilliantly in engaging with the *rhetoricity* of his texts, and thereby recreating the subtler and intenser moments in the drama of textual dialectic, that we succumb, through the persuasion of his pedagogy, to a recognition of the correspondence, or mimetic bind, in which text and reader are held. And it is this persuasion (rhetorical and dialectical at once) which alerts us to the theoretical impasse built into the project of situating the reader, namely the inability to establish a metacritical ground in which interpretations as well as a conceptual framework might be earthed. What is remarkable in this exemplary case is the apparently systematic nature of the equivocation informing the relationship of individual interpretations to a theory of understanding that aspires to metacritical status. Once again, a discontinuity or displacement between reading and its theorizations beclouds the order of reading.

In this respect it is interesting to note the uneasy rhetorical status of the theoretical manifesto 'Literature in the reader: affective stylistics', first published in 1970 and then reprinted as an appendix to the main text of *Self-Consuming Artifacts*. The position of this appendage and its relation to the body may be read as a metaphor of the equivocal relationship of reading to its object; evidently not an epilogue (the book has one, devoted to a summary of the historical thesis), its argument that 'the proper object of analysis is not the work but the reader' (p. 4) is given, as we saw, a prefatory place which is then suppressed by the emerging authority of the texts analysed. Since Fish's conceptual framework requires him to maintain both the difference between text and reader, and at the same time to assume their indivisible complicity, a Derridean logic of displacement and supplementarity begins to pervade the relationship. Thus, the appendix (its own text not free of the equivocating play of supplementarity) threatens to displace the book's central historical orientation with its deference to textual plenitude, setting up a tension that gives the book as a whole a self-subverting aspect. This aspect is even inscribed in the ambiguous genitive of the subtitle: *The Experience of Seventeenth-Century Literature.*

To recapitulate: clearly the notion of a 'dialectical' (or any other) text must remain unfulfilled without a supplementary notion of the experience of reading to constitute it. But what refuses to be resolved in Fish's project is 'the proper object of analysis'. When the reader's experience is the object of analysis, the integrity of the text is threatened; when the text becomes the focus, Fish's programme reverts to a closet formalism, in which the concept of the reader is only an extension of textual constraints or authorial intention.

Furthermore, Fish's treatment of the reader's share tends to evade the consequences of his own argument. In the first place, the ostensible role assigned to the reader keeps slipping back into a mimicry prescribed by the text. On the one hand, the text's primacy marginalizes the reader but, on the other, its own phantom fullness is made available only in a temporal process of reading consciousness. Second, the insurmountable gap or difference between direct, first-hand experience and the report of that experience implies a divided reader who can never coincide with him/herself. Third, the experience of self-consuming artefacts, contrary to all expectations, engenders a remarkably docile, singular reader who regularly acquiesces in both the rhetorical and dialectical stratagems of an apparently 'de-certainizing' yet powerfully authoritative text. The upshot of this inconclusive portrayal of the reader's role is that author, text and reader remain locked in dubious battle for the authority of meaning.

The fact that affective stylistics remains a disguised formalism is ultimately less interesting than the exemplary nature of Fish's aspiration (and failure) 'to detach the structure of the reader's experience from the formal structure of the text'

(1980, p. 136). To define the act of reading in isolation from the thing read is manifestly to espouse an unbridled subjectivism which avoids the hermeneutic structure of reading. Alternatively, a scenario postulated on the dualism of reader and text encounters the impossibility of establishing clear-cut distinctions between interpretation and fact, knower and known. New Criticism suppressed this epistemological problem. Fish restores it – to his credit – not by solving it but by proceeding to enact its problematic oscillations between reader and text in a proliferating series of displacements. Reader-response criticism thus becomes the case of a complex and interminable dialectic which persists in trying – but repeatedly fails – to negotiate the question whether reading is a transitive or intransitive verb: does the reader control the text or does the text control the reader? In his subsequent work Fish engages with the eradication of this gap or division between the contestants for the authority of literary meaning.

Is there a reader in this text?

Gaps are remarkably productive of more text, and in their wake Fish proceeded to scrutinize and challenge his own basic premises, mounting (to borrow one of his favourite verbs) a series of attacks on the positivistic assumptions – his own not excepted – of a host of theoretical projects. Between 1970 and 1980 the main plot of Fish's advocacy of reader-response criticism reached its climax and peripety in a series of publications which are now collected under the title *Is There A Text In This Class? The Authority of Interpretive Communities* (1980). In this text the seminal essay, 'Literature in the reader', resumes its primary position, inaugurating the programme to redefine literature not as an object but as something that happens when we read. In its new context, however, the force of the position adumbrated in 'Literature in the reader' serves, as Fish would have said in 1972, a 'dialectical' rather than a 'rhetorical' purpose; that is to say, it becomes the vehicle of its own overturning and abandonment in the movement towards a radically monistic view of meaning, to whose 'all-embracing unity' the procession of sequent essays presses the reader to convert.

The serial displacement or supplementation governing the development of Fish's thinking – supplanting the authority of texts by the authority of readers, in their turn supplanted by the authority of the symbolic order – represents the fundamental logical, rhetorical and thematic thrust of *Is There A Text In This Class?* Supplements galore govern the rhetorical arrangement of the occasional pieces gathered in this lively assemblage. Each essay is furnished with retrospective, self-scrutinizing and self-correcting headnotes which recreate and revaluate its role in the growth of the critic's mind, as well as providing incidental reflections on the intellectual, professional and institutional milieus and rivalries that give rise to this activity of theoretical speculation. This intensely self-conscious rhetorical disposition, throwing into relief both the internal structure of each piece, as well as its provocative relationship to its companions, invests the collection as a whole with the dramatic air and shape of a reader's *Bildungsroman*.

The narrative backbone of *Is There a Text in This Class?* charts the rise and fall of reader-response criticism from its beginnings, in the assertion of reader power, through a classical Aristotelian reversal of fortunes which puts in doubt not only the text's objectivity and the reader's autonomous selfhood but also the feasibility of the entire undertaking. It is not, however, an elegiac tale; on the contrary, the mood is consistently one of witty self-confidence and mastery, a pursuit conducted in the vigorous, jargon-free style of persuasion dear to the pragmatist Anglo-American heart. The story as I read it is a characteristic instance of the dialectic of shifting contours and perspectives which inhabit and thwart theorizations of the hermeneutic event. Stanley Fish's errant engagement with this event on behalf of the excluded reader eventually takes him far afield.

As we saw, Fish's early reader-response position implied a submerged and two-pronged intentionalism. The literary event or experience he conceptualized could be construed in two mutually exclusive senses: either it is the result of authorial intention, in which case the reader's authority becomes spurious, or it is an effect of the mind's investigation of its own activity, itself not free of intention, in which case the reader remains locked in subjectivism or solipsism. In order to resolve the residue of intentionalism, Fish's next step was to argue that

> intention and understanding are two ends of a conventional act, each of which necessarily stipulates (includes, defines, specifies) the other. To construct the profile of the informed or at-home reader is at the same time to characterize the author's intention and vice versa, because to do either is to specify the *contemporary* conditions of utterance, to identify, by becoming a member of, a community made up of those who share interpretive strategies.
>
> (1976, p. 476)

'Interpreting the *Variorum*', the essay which elaborates this argument, begins by recapitulating the thesis outlined in 'Literature in the reader', this time with reference to the critical assumptions responsible for *Variorum* compilations. According to Fish, the documentation of alternative readings of textual cruxes creates the false impression that these cruxes exist to be solved rather than to be experienced; 'consequently any procedure that attempts to determine which of a number of readings is correct will necessarily fail' (1976, p. 465). With this in mind, he examines several examples of points in dispute in Milton's sonnets, from which he proceeds to conclude that the textual phenomena under consideration – 'formal units' such as line endings, an ambiguous piece of language, puns, etc. – are not objective and autonomous facts embedded in the text but are always already the result of our perceptual strategies, our reading acts. From the assumption that we begin with an interpretation already in place, it follows that there is no pre-existing text which controls the reader's response: our 'texts' are our readings, the poems we 'write'. The dazzlingly simple thrust of this thesis enables Fish to subsume both Affective and Intentional Fallacies in a gesture of transcendence which spirals to a point above them.

> This, then, is my thesis: that the form of the reader's experience, formal units, and the structure of intention are one, that they come into view simultaneously, and that therefore questions of priority and independence do not arise. What does arise is another question: what produces

them? That is, if intention, form, and the shape of the reader's experience are simply different ways of referring to (different perspectives on) the same interpretive act, what is that act an interpretation *of*? I cannot answer that question, but neither, I would claim, can anyone else, although formalists try to answer it by pointing to patterns and claiming that they are available independently of (prior to) interpretation. These patterns vary according to the procedures that yield them . . . but whatever they are I would argue they do not lie innocently in the world but are themselves constituted by an interpretive act.

(1976, p. 479)

The elegant streamlining of this model may be seen as the apotheosis of Fish's undersong, which, as I read it, is a suite of variations on the yearning for the ultimate authority of a unifying centre. It is as though the self-transcending impulse of the 'dialectical' texts described in *Self-Consuming Artifacts* is now canonized in a comprehensive metatheory of literary understanding which proposes that we drop our hierarchical views of the structure governing the relationship between author, text, and reader, collapsing this classical trinity into a single, egalitarian simultaneity, beyond genetic or causal distinctions. To specify any one term along the axis of communication is to specify all the rest, for they are all absorbed into a higher authority:

meanings are the property neither of fixed and stable texts nor of free and independent readers but of interpretive communities that are responsible both for the shape of the reader's activities and for the texts those activities produce.

(1980, p. 322)

By 'interpretive communities' Fish does not mean a collective of individuals but a bundle of strategies or norms of interpretation that we hold in common and which regulate the way we think and perceive. In other words, Fish now subscribes to the semiological interpretive community discussed in the previous chapter which holds that our categories of perception are not unique, individual or idio-syncratic, but conventional and communal. Encoded in language, institutionalized, already in place, they exist prior to the act of reading.

The surprising but necessary outcome of this attack on the independence of textual meaning is to undermine not only the formalist position but also the grounds for reader-response criticism as an alternative project. 'At a stroke', Fish's unitary model neutralizes 'the dilemma that gave rise to the debate between the champions of the text and the champions of the reader' (1980, p. 14). Indeed, the opposition of subject and object ceases to be relevant when reader and text are made to disappear into discursive systems of intelligibility, systems which are not a reflection of reality, but are that which is responsible for the 'reality' of readers and texts. And without a subject/object opposition, reader-response criticism also disappears at a stroke, for if 'the self does not exist apart from the communal or conventional categories of thought that enable its operations (of thinking, seeing, reading)' (1980, p. 335), then *a fortiori* there is no primary consciousness to function as the locus of meaning. The reader's self is itself a sign – another text.[5] Like 'formal units', it is what our critical conventions allow us to perceive. What also 'disappears at a stroke' is the entire dyadic structure on which traditional distinctions of literary discourse are founded – distinctions such as those between ordinary and poetic language, or scientific and emotive language, form and content, description and interpretation, intrinsic and extrinsic, etc. One consequence of the eradication of these distinctions is a subversion of the accounts of literary representation which follow from them. If the language of poetry is not a deviation from standard or ordinary language, but is that which comes into view when one places a particular interpretive frame around language, then the distinction which stylisticians, for example, make between form and content or description and interpretation is purely arbitrary. Stylistics, therefore, is *in principle* a theoretically incoherent project, which continues to thrive only because its assumptions are ignored or suppressed by the community of its practitioners (see 'What is stylistics and why are they saying such terrible things about it?', I and II, reprinted in Fish, 1980).

Where then is meaning *made* and what is the nature of the

knowledge derived from reading a poem? The answer to this question is elusive. When meaning is defined as neither subjective act nor objective fact, it 'necessarily eludes critical location', as William Ray points out (1984, p. 164). But for Fish, this elusiveness quite emphatically does not lead to negative hermeneutics or to a deconstructionist 'universe of absolute free play in which everything is indeterminate and undecidable' (1980, p. 268). On the contrary, meaning for him is always determinate and decidable because it is constrained by and built into a context of interpretation. The reader, who is at once interpreter and interpretation, is always situated inside a system of language, inside a context of discursive practices in which are inscribed values, interests, attitudes, beliefs. In Fish's view, for example, the import of speech–act theory is that a system of language cannot be characterized in isolation from a context of discursive circumstances which situate us. Each and every instance of consciousness or utterance is framed by a specific situation. A reader, like a sentence, is

> never not in a context. We are never not in a situation. A statute is never not read in the light of some purpose. A set of interpretive assumptions is always in force. A sentence that seems to need no interpretation is already the product of one. . . . No sentence is ever apprehended independently of some or other illocutionary force.

> (1978, p. 637)

Meaning, therefore, is always readily available; and it is brought to light not as the perplexed process of (mis)understanding that constitutes the hermeneutic dialogue but rather as an act of rhetorical persuasion inviting our assent to a set of beliefs. 'Indeed', Fish declares, 'this is the whole of critical activity, an attempt on the part of one party to alter the beliefs of another so that the evidence cited by the first will be seen *as* evidence by the second' (1980, p. 365). What is disturbing is the fact that the explanatory force of Fish's model for the 'whole' of critical activity achieves its masterful stance by outflanking impatiently the problem of understanding. Excluded by this model of institutionalized reading is the enabling fiction of the moment of consciousness we think of as self-knowledge (or -doubt or negativity). Without that fiction, what *difference*, we might ask, does reading make? Fish's subject, imprisoned in communal norms of interpretation and coerced by their authority, has no means of engaging with the more recalcitrant features of texts, with their rhetoricity, with the infinite regress of figuration, with doubt, uncertainty, or irony, with the strangeness and 'otherness' of poetry or language.[6] He can only appropriate them blindly as the already available terms for naturalizing meaning. He cannot even know the present conditions of his knowing or his blindness; he can only repeat them. And he will repeat them without anguish or anxiety, for in a belief-centred orientation the reader never stumbles or loses his balance – there is always the net of another convention to catch his fall.

Given this theoretical position, a radical retreat from reading ensues. In the first place, there are no practical pedagogical or methodological consequences to Fish's position: the Fishian reader is encouraged to continue exercising the literary competence of 'informed' reading bequeathed by the institution in which he is trained. This is no longer because reader-response criticism has any claims to be a superior or more valid methodology – it is but one of any number of interpretive strategies – but because it survives by default. Moreover, not only does reader-response theory disappear, but all literary theory as such loses its specificity in the progressive engulfment in socio-cultural questions of professionalism, politics and institutional power.[7] But the ramifications of these questions of power and authority cannot be seriously engaged if the activity of reading is denied its powers of resisting, reinventing, revising, understanding the texts of power and authority. If, theoretically, everything is enabled by institutional assumptions, then the end of criticism, as Fish would have it, is reduced to no more than a gesture of persuasion which dangerously trivializes the vigilant travail of reading: trivializes, because reading, if conceptualized (interpreted) as a foregone, conservative submission to authority, will reproduce blindness without insight; dangerously, because Fish's position so far has refused to face up to the ways in which the authority of interpretive communities might become grimly coercive. The salutary curb on subjectivity, without a corresponding curb on the authority of consensual norms, remains troubling. The appeal to the imperialism of agreement can chill the spines of readers whose experience of the community is less happily benign than Fish assumes.

5
The relation of the reader to daydreaming: Norman Holland and transactive criticism

scooped out
By help of dreams . . .

(Wordsworth, *Home at Grasmere*)

One predictable turn taken by the disaffection with a supposedly impersonal ideal of literary criticism was in the direction of psychoanalytic criticism whose promise to uncover new areas of the self combined with the renascent interest in readers and the reading process.

> The literary critic comes to psychoanalysis because psycho-analysis promises to tell him something about people. Psychoanalysis has nothing, nothing whatsoever, to tell us about literature per se. But psychoanalysis, particularly in its theories of character, has a great deal to tell us about people engaged in literature, either writing it or reading it or being portrayed in it.
>
> (Holland 1982, p. 31)

This surprisingly precipitate statement by Norman Holland, the subject of this chapter and the leading proponent of a psychoanalytic approach to reader-response criticism, betrays the uneasy sense of discontinuity and asymmetry which has haunted the coupling of psychoanalysis and literary analysis in traditional Anglo-American psychoaesthetic ventures. It would not be unfair to say that on some very general level Holland speaks for the powerful and influential mainstream attitude to the subject. The correspondence or sympathy between psychoanalysis and literary analysis is frequently acknowledged only to be rapidly confined to the realm of 'people' rather than 'literature' as though to deny or bracket the question of the inextricable entanglement of human experience in linguistic symbolization.

My point is of course grossly reductive, as any history of the relationship between these two modes of interpretation will reveal, yet this history, from its Freudian inauguration, has arguably been attended by a recurrent imbalance. One prominent feature of this imbalance can be traced in the attitude which takes for granted the competence and preroga-tive of psychoanalysis to teach literature something about itself and its unconscious motives, whereas literature is granted little or nothing to teach psychoanalysis about itself. It is only recently that this asymmetry has been observed and challenged by both literary critics and psychoanalysts who are rediscover-ing and re-emphasizing the literary and textual nature of psychoanalytic knowledge. Under the impact of Jacques Lacan's revisionary reading of Freud, for example, we are learning to read the unconscious 'like a language' in which the sign ('letter' or 'character') is the symbol of a lack or absence (Lacan 1972). This interesting development in the history of psychoanalysis has opened up the possibility of 're-inventing', as Shoshana Felman puts it, the mutual relationship of literary analysis and psychoanalysis as the demarcation of a site or *topos* of reading. Rather than subordinate one discipline and risk its assimilation into the other, the new reciprocity aspires to subvert the erstwhile master–slave relationship by showing how 'in the same way that psychoanalysis points to the unconscious of literature, *literature, in its turn, is the unconscious of psychoanalysis*' (Felman 1977, p. 10).

Since psychoanalytically oriented reader-response criticism (and Holland's in particular) has declared its allegiance to people and to the assumptions of American ego-psychology and object-relations theory,[1] and has preferred to avoid the crucial Lacanian complication (more crucial, perhaps, for the fortunes of criticism than clinical practice), it seems all the more necessary to remind ourselves, no matter how cursorily, of the existence of a contemporary juncture of concerns which all invoke the honoured name of Freud in conjunction with a psychoanalytic reading practice. Today such a practice frequently performs a double movement: side by side with the more traditional methods of reading the literary text in the light of psychoanalytic knowledge, it also solicits a reading of the psychoanalytic text in the light of literary knowledge.

The daydreamer: analyst or analysand?

Let me begin with an allegory of reading to illustrate my introductory remarks. Among Freud's intermittent contributions to aesthetics, one widely anthologized piece is the essay of 1908 entitled 'Creative writers and daydreaming'. This cheerful essay – an offshoot of Freud's march to the unconscious along the 'royal road' of dreams – suggests a promising trail for affective criticism; for what Freud claims to uncover are the psychological motives underlying both the creative and the receptive process. Essentially these processes coincide in an unconscious complicity between reader and writer to transform fantasy or unconscious wish into pleasure. Here is Freud's conclusion:

> How the writer accomplishes this [our pleasure in his work] is his innermost secret; the essential *ars poetica* lies in the technique of overcoming the feeling of repulsion in us which is undoubtedly connected with the barriers that rise between each single ego and the others. We can guess two of the methods used by this technique. The writer softens the character of his egoistic daydreams by altering and disguising it, and he bribes us by the purely formal – that is, aesthetic – yield of pleasure which he offers us in the presentation of his fantasies. We give the name of an *incentive bonus*, or a *fore-pleasure*, to a yield of pleasure such as this, which is offered to us so as to make possible the release of still greater pleasure arising from deeper psychical sources. In my opinion, all the aesthetic pleasure which a creative writer affords us has the character of a fore-pleasure of this

kind, and our actual enjoyment of an imaginative work proceeds from a liberation of tensions in our minds. It may even be that not a little of this effect is due to the writer's enabling us thenceforward to enjoy our own day-dreams without self-reproach or shame. This brings us to the threshold of new, interesting and complicated enquiries; but also, at least for the moment, to the end of our discussion.

(1953, p. 153)

The truth about our reading, Freud suggests, lies in the benign collusion of readers and writers to disguise the truth about their (our) egoism, in order to achieve pleasure. These latent motives can be brought to light by shrewd analysis.

Let us suppose, however, that the disclosure of a hidden motive does not bring us face to face with the 'truth' but serves to veil some other motive. The circuitous rhetorical path by which Freud leads us to his concluding insight in the essay could then be interpreted to suggest some other, equally oblique, and possibly darker tale, one in which, for instance, the destinies of writers and readers/analysts converge in a struggle for priority. I shall attempt to outline this hypothetical alternative sub-text as a brief prologue to the story of reading psychoanalytically.

The organizing principle of Freud's essay is one of analogy, a rhetorical procedure which generates a proliferating and suggestive play of doublings and displacements. Just as the child at play, Freud tells us, creates a world of fantasy distinct from 'reality', so the adult, be he the successful artist or the unhappy neurotic, creates fantasies and daydreams distinct from – and indeed often in conflicting relationship to – the facts of 'real' life. Adult daydreaming and fantasizing are a disguised continuation or displacement of play, but because playing is childish, and fantasizing indulges in socially and culturally shameful or prohibited thoughts, these activities must retreat into guileful secrecy. Now the dynamics of fantasizing, Freud says, are analogous to nocturnal dreams; that is to say, 'the motive forces of phantasies are unsatisfied wishes and every single phantasy is the fulfillment of a wish' (p. 146). The same is true of the literary work which is a disguised and stealthy enactment of a daydream in which 'past, present and future are strung together, as it were, on the thread of the wish that runs through them' (p. 148). Lurking behind it we can always detect 'His Majesty the Ego, the hero of every daydream and every story' (p. 150).

As one scrutinizes the essay for more than its psychoanalytic information, it begins to emerge that the thrust of Freud's analogizing manifestly devalues, even cancels out, the 'strangeness', the singularity, specificity and rareness of the poetic power whose genesis was the original object of Freud's speculations. It would seem that Freud is of two minds with regard to poets. On the one hand he grants poets an originary and mysterious power of imagination; but on the other hand he slyly subverts that image by pointing out that their naïve motives are all too transparent to the perceptions of the shrewd analyst, himself a powerful writer and the founder of a formidable method of probing the mysteries of the human mind. But why should Freud be employing his considerable rhetorical skills to subvert the prestige of the creative writer by a stark exposure of the egotistical character of all writing? What is at stake in Freud's condensed reflection upon the origins and originality of the literary work? Are we in the presence of a case of sibling rivalry (and Freud's remark that the poets were there before him springs to mind)? To put it even more bluntly and tendentiously, who is the 'hero' or subject of Freud's essay?

If the object of a writer's desire may be inferred by its displacement into his text, then the object of Freud's desire may, by virtue of the same Freudian insight, be inferred from its displacement into the subject of his essay. Consider, for example, the rhetorical gesture announcing Freud's 'daydream'; it occurs very near the beginning of the essay and is identical with the move which announces the analogical procedure of inferences followed in the development of his hypothesis.

> If we could at least discover in ourselves, or in people like ourselves, an activity which was in some way akin to creative writing! An examination of it would then give us a hope of obtaining the beginnings of an explanation of the creative work of writers. And, indeed, there is some prospect

of this being possible. After all, creative writers themselves like to lessen the distance between their kind and the common run of humanity; they so often assure us that every man is a poet at heart

(p. 143)

Note the elasticity of the shifter: does the pronoun 'we' designate the author? Or an intimate community of analysts? Or a much broader community of common readers?[2] In Freud's optative mood distinctions between readers and writers, subject and object, analyst and analysand, begin to shift and blur. What complicates the identity of the subject of Freud's essay considerably is the infolding of empirical subject and theoretical object within a single strategy of reading. Freud, in this instance, turns out to be not of two minds but of *three*. Reading the Freudian text rhetorically, that is to say against itself, alerts us to the ways in which its narrative strategy implicates the author–narrator in a triangular drama of what René Girard calls mimetic rivalry by casting him in a complicated triple role. Occupying the positions of analyst, writer, and reader, the figure of 'Freud' is a paradoxical site of convergences and displacements: at once the analyst–physician or objective scientist in pursuit of the true principles governing creativity and receptivity; *and* the writer and creator of an entirely original story about the making of stories; *and* the subjective reader whose speculations upon literature and the reading experience provide the introspective grounds for the story of reading with whose happy ending the essay concludes (not without promise of further ventures and discoveries). These roles are so inextricably enmeshed and contaminated that we are unable to say how literally we ought to take Freud's allegory of reading. To what extent can His Majesty the Ego neutralize his inescapably egotistical character so as to present an impartial and scientifically objective account of his ego-dominated reading and writing? But of course this question can only be posed – indeed, must be posed, even if it cannot be satisfactorily answered – because we already stand within the site cleared by Freud.

But I shall here suspend further reflection upon the question of how we read *with* and *against* Freud, and how we construe the disconcerting relationship between Freud's daydream and his science (indeed, his dream of science), and turn to Norman Holland's application of Freudian theory in the construction of an aesthetics of response.

'His Majesty the Ego'

Norman Holland's project begins by contextualizing itself firmly and unquestioningly within classical Freudian terms. In a sense it could be said to undertake the task of writing a sequel to Freud's manifest narrative of the creative and receptive process.

As Holland sees it, the transformation of fantasy material into socially acceptable meanings is what both literature and its readings are all about. Beginning with the view that art's formal properties and the reader's pleasure in them are a reconciliation between the competing pressures of impulse and inhibition, Holland focuses on the centrality of the ego's mediating activities between the urge to fulfil desire and the necessity of coping with reality. Over a number of years he has constructed a model of reading based on the notion that reading is a dynamic *transaction* between the formal properties of the textual object, and the defensive strategies of individual consciousness. Thus, in *The Dynamics of Literary Response* (1968), Holland set himself the task of constructing a theoretical model which would account for 'the relation between the patterns [the critic] finds objectively in the text and the reader's subjective experience of the text' (p. xiii), with a view to integrating the close study of texts with close study of the human mind. The informing premise is that 'literature is an objective text, but also a subjective experience' (p. 108).

In many essentials, Holland's efforts to effect a theoretical alliance between New Critical literary analysis and psychoanalysis are strongly influenced by the ego-psychology of Freud's disciple, Ernst Kris, according to whose aesthetic theory artistic form is an expression of the ego's successful harnessing of the explosive energies of desire inhabiting the id. The ego patrols the boundary between conscious and unconscious, relaxing or tightening control in accordance with its needs. 'Central to artistic – or indeed, any other – creativeness is a relaxation ("regression") of ego functions. . . . But the regression in the case of aesthetic creation is purposive and controlled' (Kris 1964, first published 1952, p. 253). When Kris, with Empson's *Seven Types of Ambiguity* in mind, compares aesthetic ambiguity with overdetermination (the mode by which the unconscious attaches a multiplicity of meanings to one particular image or symptom), it is in order to argue that the ego safely manages and directs the unbound, disjunctive and subversive energies of primary process towards coherence and publicly shareable significance. We can easily detect in Kris's analogy Freud's paradigmatic art/(day)dream analogy. The work of art reproduces material from the unconscious but it censors and 'softens' this material by means of the distortions and distractions we think of as literary devices, so as to defend against the threat of exposure.

How do we read with and through the defences of literature and of our own psychic makeup?[3] Literature, in Holland's view, is a secondary-process activity of 'transformation', and its meaning is 'analogous to the sublimation of an infantile fantasy' (1968, p. 12). In conventional formalist criticism, literary meaning is discovered by showing how all the elements in a text relate to a governing and informing idea. But from a psychoanalytic perspective literary meaning is constituted in the dynamic process of transforming an unconscious fantasy into intellectual terms.

To illustrate this hypothesis, Holland analyses 'The Wife of Bath's Tale', using the standard New Critical mode of analysis to show how the formal elements of Chaucer's narrative are organized around the central idea of 'maistrie', an idea represented in that text by a series of events which dramatizes contests between principles of male and female authority, or of dominance versus submission. These representations, Holland then argues, defend against a submerged or unconscious fantasy of phallic wounding or oral wounding: 'the Tale starts with phallic, aggressive sexuality [a knight rapes a maiden and is condemned to death unless he can correctly tell "what thing is it that wommen most desiren"] regresses to a more primitive relation between taboo mother and passive son [the knight marries the disgusting old crone who promises to give him the

life-saving answer] and finally progresses to genital mutuality'
(p. 16). The unconscious drama reaches its happy formal
resolution when the knight succumbs to his loathly lady's
'maistrie'. She offers him the choice between herself as old and
foul but true, or herself as young and beautiful but unfaithful.
The Tale's happy ending rewards his choice of the old crone
with a wife both young and true. Thus the story, in Holland's
reading, transforms the anxiety of an unconscious infantile
fantasy shared by the reader ('if I am phallicly aggressive and
do not submit to my mother she will castrate me' (p. 27)), into
socially, morally and intellectually acceptable and pleasurable
terms. By means of a complex interaction and matching of the
reader's and the text's 'defenses', primitive wishes and fears
are metamorphosed into 'significance and coherence' (p. 30).

Holland ascribes to this process of transformation the status
of a general truth about all literary texts and their reception:
poems or narratives always transform an unconscious core
fantasy, disguising, repressing or sublimating it in a manner
which yields gratification. (An entire chapter of *The Dynamics of
Literary Response* is devoted to a 'dictionary' of such fantasies,
following the Freudian psychosexual phases – oral, anal,
phallic and genital – of infantile development.) 'Consciously
. . . we give or find in the text "meaning" by a process of
successive abstraction and classification from the words and
events of the text. Unconsciously, we introject the text and feel
its nuclear fantasy as though it were our own unconscious
fantasy – yet we are not aware of it as such' (p. 180).
According to this pattern, that which conventional literary
criticism calls 'content' corresponds to fantasy or impulse (the
'latent' content of psychoanalytic parlance), whilst aesthetic
form – the array of formal rhetorical devices, the 'manifest'
content – is the equivalent of psychic defence. And just as form
and content are inseparable so impulse and defence interact
and shape each other. The partnership between literary
analysis and psychoanalysis finds its *raison d'être* in the
dynamic interaction which prompts the reader to make use of
his own unconscious response in order to perceive what is
going on within the text whilst experiencing that response as
another's (i.e. the text's). It follows that reading psychoanalytically enables us to discover both the text's deepest

sources of meaning, as well as our (unconscious) selves, our own 'otherness'.

One could surmise how such an encounter may well threaten to undermine any assumption of the ego's confident wholeness or self-possession, but in Holland's version of this process the reader's encounter with 'otherness' is notably light-hearted and tediously predictable. Ultimately free of guilt, shame, or the fear of disintegration, reading, in this account, takes place within a hedonistic economy in which defensive actions are reinforced with 'multiple bonuses of pleasure':

> In life, defenses stand off and modify drives and so cut down the amount of pleasure we get even if the drives are gratified. If however, the defense itself gives pleasure, there is a net increase in pleasure, and that increase in pleasure (according to Freud) buys a permit for 'a still greater pleasure arising from deeper psychical sources,' the gratification from the drive (or, in literature, unconscious content). Thus, even the pleasure from satisfying the drive becomes greater. It is as though a kind of multiplier came into play like those in economics, so that a little pleasure in form releases a far greater pleasure in content.
>
> (p. 132)

In Holland's account of the calculus which governs the literary transaction there are only gains to be reckoned – and the recurrent metaphors of 'addition', 'combination' and 'multiplication' in his theorizing privilege the entrepreneur's concern with the profits and losses of 'pleasure', rather than the exegete's anxiety about the risks of critical 'understanding'.

Holland's determination to convert psychic misery into determinate and computable returns of psychic and aesthetic pleasure or control is well exemplified in an extended reading (pp. 106–14) of the 'Tomorrow, and tomorrow, and tomorrow' speech in *Macbeth* (V.v.19–28). Taking a New Critical reading of this text (J.C. Ransom's remarks to the effect that although dramatically powerful, the imagery renders the speech discontinuous and incoherent) as his jumping-off point, Holland out-Herods the formalist Herod's prosecution of unity and closure by uncovering the coherence of the 'unconscious content'. The images, he tells us,

> act out a going to bed followed by frightening imaginings associated with adult activities, namely, a stage play . . . [T]here is a well-documented and well-nigh universal unconscious meaning to dreams and fantasies of watching stage performances. They signify a child's fantasies of watching what he takes to be the sadistic, bloody violence of his parents in the struggle of love ending in a death-like sleep
>
> (pp. 110–11 – and a footnote refers us to Freud, 'On the sexual theories of children')

The strutting player in the role of father, the phallic 'brief candle' which must 'out', an imagined tale 'full of sound and fury' – these images and others in the text, Holland claims, enact a bi-fold impulse to see and not to see the performance; hence the presence of the rhetorical defence strategies of 'denial' as well as the shift from sight to sound. The dynamics of response, according to Holland, lead from the text's conscious level of tension, strife, and despair to an unconscious level of frightening childish imaginings (shared by the reader), yet also to an abatement of anxiety in the reassurance that these events signify 'nothing'. (An examination of Matthew Arnold's 'Dover Beach' in the same chapter predictably yields very similar results.)

Even if for the moment we discount doubts regarding the 'universality' of such meanings, the question still remains whether the reassuring securities of converting trauma into pleasure have not slackened the more strenuous labours of understanding the figurative power of language. It is the confident glossing of verbal representation into the determinate reductions of Freudian orthodoxy that has given psychoanalytic criticism a bad name, as Frederick Crews has pointed out. Instead of being illuminated by psychoanalytic terms, the text's specificity is simply sacrificed to the interpretive scheme, and literary meaning is confined to a meagre repertoire of predictable infantile fantasies: 'find the devouring mother, detect the inevitable castration anxiety, listen, between the syllables of verse, for the squeaking bedsprings of the primal

scene' (Crews 1975, p. 166). All the voyeuristic reader is
allowed is the rather passive role of reshuffling the counters
provided by his dictionary of fantasies.

The question of whose fantasies they are remains suspended.
The postulate of universality allows Holland to evade the
question of whose consciousness or unconscious – whether
Shakespeare's, Macbeth's or the reader's – qualifies as the
generative source of the primal fantasy. The understanding
that the bedtime fantasy is somehow embedded in the text
itself corresponds to Holland's fidelity to New Critical
principles. To be sure, the recognition that reading has a
psychology and that the subjectivity of reading is a constitutive
part of the aesthetic experience is in itself a significant and
original departure from New Critical orthodoxy. But the
solidly objectivist residue which underwrites the combination
of two positivistic strains (the doctrines of the text's objectivity
and the ego's autonomy) in Holland's model undoes the
intended concession to subjectivity. And even when in his
subsequent work Holland adopts the view that texts are
merely 'marks on a page' (1975a, p. 14) which in and of
themselves have no meaning, and abandons the hypothesis
that texts have fantasies – only people do – he implicitly
continues to reify the objective text and the autonomous self.
His incomplete and contradictory account of subjectivity
remains, as we shall see, the central difficulty in the revised
model of transactive criticism to which I now turn.

Transactive criticism

According to Holland's new transactive paradigm, the reader
uses the literary text to enact his basic compulsion not only to
produce a centring and unifying interpretation of experience,
but, more specifically, to recreate himself, his own identity.
The 'inanimate' literary work is 'not a work in itself but the
occasion for some person's work (in the sense we give the word
when we speak of the "dream-work" or creative "work")'
(1975a, p. 17). This work of converting the text into socially,
morally and intellectually acceptable meanings is determined
by the reader's personality. Over the question of the text's
objective status Holland remains noncommittal but implicitly

he continues to reify the 'marks on the page' as an objectively available 'promptuary' which 'includes constraints on how one can put its contents together' (p. 286).

The gist of Holland's thesis, distilled and reiterated with evangelical zeal over recent years and numerous publications, holds that '*interpretation is a function of identity*' (1975b, p. 816). As a woman/man is so she/he reads. A literary transaction has the same dialectical structure as our other acts of perception: we perceive the text, as we perceive all reality, through a pre-existing schema: 'each of us will find in the literary work the kind of thing we characteristically wish or fear the most' (p. 817). We take in from the work that which our adaptive strategies permit, and we derive from it fantasies of the kind that give us pleasure. The modality of response is determined by our 'identity theme', a notion of selfhood which Holland borrows from the ego psychologist Hans Lichtenstein, and which postulates our possession of a continuing and constant core of personality, 'an unchanging essence . . . that permeates the millions of ego choices that constitute the visible human before me' (p. 815). This individual and personal 'style' of coping with experience is constituted by a person's characteristic configuration of defences, expectations, fantasies, and transformations (a gestalt for which Holland coins the acronym **DEFT**) through which each new experience is filtered in an ongoing process of adaptation and assimilation. The purpose of this process is to replicate the reader's enduring sameness, his core identity theme – rather like a melody, to quote Holland's favourite comparison, on which an infinity of variations can be played out (p. 814).

Holland tested his new intuitions empirically in an extended experimental programme (in some ways a psychologically updated elaboration of Richards's protocols experiment), whose results are copiously described in *5 Readers Reading* (1975a). Puzzled by the persistent divergences and idiosyncrasies of different readers' responses to the stimulus of the 'same' text, he undertook to analyse taped interviews of students' responses to Faulkner's 'A Rose for Emily', and found that these responses did not match his own psychoanalytic reading of this text, but that they *did* conform to his analyses of the readers' personalities (obtained by means of psychological tests such as Rorschach and Thematic Apperception Tests). It was the results he came up with that led him to redefine his earlier transactive model of reading on the deceptively simple lines of personality as the determinant of reading. A sizeable portion of *5 Readers Reading* is devoted to an analysis of the recorded comments and thoughts of Sandra, Sam, Shep, Saul and Sebastian, the protagonists of Holland's story of reading, who are analysed for their 'identity themes' with the same scrupulous and worrying attention which any respectable New Critic confers on a poem.

Interpretation, according to this 'transactive' model, is a process of recreating the 'text' (meaningless in itself), according to the shape determined by the magnetic field of the reader's identity theme. Meaning is not of or about or in the text but of and about readers, be they Holland's personality-tested subjects, or canonical writers such as Robert Frost (1975), Dr Johnson (1978), H.D (1973) or Holland himself (1980). The novelty of the model lies in its large-scale licensing of the intrusion of biographical materials. Interpretation, willy-nilly, becomes a confessional mode (see Holland 1976, 1980).

The force of Holland's model – its obvious, commonsensical and ultimately trivial characterology – is also its great weakness. Empirically, most of us tend to think of ourselves and others in terms of distinctive and recognizable 'styles' which integrate and unify different aspects and details of our behaviour into recurrent patterns. To exchange this humanist persuasion for a theory of 'absence' or self-division is to perform a move as counter-intuitive as abandoning the concept of an objective, self-identical text. This Holland is reluctant to do: and the adherence to his 'humanist' persuasions even when his theory undercuts them opens a gap between theory and practice. In effect his strategy in all his case histories of reader-response is to shift the unity and self-identity, traditionally attributed to the autonomous text, from the literary work to the text of a reader's 'self'. The formula, '*Unity* is to *text* as *identity* is to *self*' (1975b, p. 815), braids psychoanalytic and literary concepts, in order to indicate that 'unity' and 'identity' represent the 'invariables' from which the 'variables' of 'text' and 'self' are derived. But the neat symmetry is deceptive, and collapses under scrutiny. This is evident in Holland's own failure to use his terminology consistently, as when he is led to claim that the variables 'text' and 'self' show sameness as well as difference, or when he slides into a usage of 'self' and 'identity' as interchangeable synonyms. Basically, the model totters over its inability to decide whether the 'self' is the provisional product of interpretation or an 'unchanging essence'. This is due to the fact that Holland seems unable to shake off the empirical conviction that the 'self', like the text, is an objective or real entity, a conviction reinforced by his analyses of real readers the impression of whose abiding 'personality' serves as the key to an explanation of their reading practices.

Holland never joins battle directly with the structuralist or Lacanian alternative which rejects conceptualizations of the ego as a reified product of its imaginary identifications in favour of a 'subject' inserted in and constituted by the pre-existing symbolic order of language. A *locus classicus* for this alternative view is Lacan's famous seminar on 'The Purloined Letter' around which a little canon of commentary has grown.[4] Lacan uses Poe's story as a fable of analysis in which the 'letter' (punning on typographical character and epistle) represents the operations of the signifier, a unit of signification without inherent meaning. The 'letter' (the contents of the letter are never revealed) is that which everyone aspires to possess but is also that which remains perpetually out of reach, representing an irrecoverable lack. What is available to the reader/analyst is not a meaning but an arrangement, a chain of figurations or symbolic displacements, a structure of exchange that charts the path that the signifier travels. To read is to enter and repeat the structures of the signifying chain rather than to appropriate a meaning. Holland's counter-statement to Lacan – in 'Re-covering "The Purloined Letter" ', a piece written for the anthology of reader- and audience-oriented criticism edited by Susan R. Suleiman (1980) – declares his humanist belief that texts and reading practices should be saved from the Lacanian and Derridean threat. 'We can restore stories to their rightful owners – you and me and all of you and me, our emotional as well as our intellectual selves – by recovering reading as a personal transaction' (p. 370). But his 'small skirmish' (p. 362) with Lacan and Derrida covers up the area of disagreement by avoiding any real engagement with the Lacanian position. In its stead, Holland offers one more exposition of the transactive paradigm, using Poe's story as the pretext for the free-associating and candidly personal responses invited by the transactive method. If in the Lacanian analysis the conduct of the signifier represents a lack or absence which precludes illusions of possession, self-possession and plenitude, for Holland the plenitude of the reader's self is axiomatic. The story's central motif (the hiding and revealing of secrets and texts) calls into play a transaction between the tale's and the reader's textual/sexual concerns; this prompts Holland to confront his own relationship to secrets both adolescent (e.g. a 13-year-old Holland masturbating) and adult (a 52-year-old Holland daydreaming of professional rivalry and mastery). Holland's strategy (or fantasy) to 'outwit' (p. 356) the professional 'fathers' (Lacan and Derrida), by suggesting that their infatuation with absence and scepticism conceals a nostalgia for presence and trust, avoids an exposure of his own position to the critique of selfhood which the structuralist and post-structuralist positions pursue. The rival positions are aligned but the actual engagement (which might reveal, for instance, that each is the other's repressed twin) does not occur.

Holland's model has been variously attacked for resting on a faulty and misconceived epistemology. Holland himself tends to steer clear of philosophical issues and prevaricates over his ontological premises regarding the existence of a unitary and stable self or text, but the unacknowledged outcome is a distinct reification which neither contemporary metapsychology nor literary criticism in the wake of semiotics will bear out. As with the notion of 'self' Holland conveniently allows himself to forget that 'identity' is not a uniform or monolithic substance but an indeterminate sign or a verbal representation, a concept which is the product of our linguistic practices rather than their cause. It can therefore be argued, as Jonathan Culler has done, that the 'free' associations of Sandra, Shep *et al.* reveal not their unique individuality but 'the clichés of the various subcultures and cultural discourses that work to constitute the consciousness of American college students' (1981, p. 53). Furthermore, on Holland's own terms, these 'selves', like the texts they read, cannot be described independently of the analyst's identity. The resulting circularity confines interpretation to an intrasubjective repetition which can have no objectively valid explanatory power with respect to its object.

As William Ray cogently formulates it, the epistemological problem with Holland's procedure lies in its 'render[ing] the identity theme of the subject in question inseparable from that of the critic who describes it' (1984, p. 67). The possibility of understanding a text is thereby undermined since, in Holland's own terms, *any* text will inevitably be a self-replication, his own not excluded. It is precisely the predicament of where and how to situate 'the subject in question' that leads to the critical aporia. The possibility of understanding a 'text' fares no better than the 'self' (and the reified self which is Holland's subject is always already a text) because Holland's 'readings' of readers can only be, according to this principle, the inescapable self-replications of Holland's own identity theme. Theoretically speaking, when the reader and the read occupy the same site (call it 'subjectivity'), the transaction faces the impasse of swallowing its own tail – a predicament also dramatized in the Freudian allegory of reading with which I began this chapter. What, then, is the status and authority of a discourse which marches under the standard of subjectivity if all interpretation (a category which – broad enough to encompass the literary text, the spontaneous oral utterances of students, the analyst's metacritical discourse – leaves out little of linguistic usage) repeats only the interpreter's ego *ad infinitum*? Whilst such a discourse collapses the disabling opposition of subject and object, it also excludes itself, *ipso facto*, from claims of truth and objective knowledge by falling into an abyss of infinite regress. Under such conditions, what knowledge, if any, can be educed?

Holland's reply to this objection resorts rather feebly to a mystifying rhetoric of long addition sums. In 'How can Dr Johnson's remarks on Cordelia's death add to my own response?' (1978) he argues that Johnson's reading of *King Lear* can be seen as a function of Johnson's identity theme (which, according to Holland, characteristically takes the shape of a regular confrontation and balancing of competing claims and forces); but Johnson's reading of the play is also 'dialectical'(?), insofar as it is a transaction between himself and the text, as well as himself and other readers. Add to that Holland's own reading of Johnson's reading, and the possibilities for input grow infinite. For Holland, all this baroque algebra provides the option to capitalize on and amplify a hoard of readings, and what saves the model from infinite regress, he claims, are the principles of DEFT and Freudian aesthetics which can be counted on to ground us (p. 40). But it is difficult to say that the argument has earned its right to move from a solipsistic loop of intrasubjective transaction to a more intersubjective hermeneutic.

More recently (1982) Holland has appealed loosely to the phenomenon of 'transference' as an explanation of the transactive dynamics of reading. Transference is the inevitable and necessary process which occurs in the analyst's consulting room when the analysand unconsciously reproduces repressed emotions and experiences, substituting the person of the analyst for the original object of the repressed impulse. This process is complicated by counter-transference (from analyst to analysand) when the analyst's unconscious response joins the analysand's in a mutual playing out of subjectivities. A transferential model would allow us to take as the object of analysis not the text or the reader alone, but reading itself, thus circumventing the problem of mastery in the analytic space. If the encounter of analyst and analysand is seen to correspond to the encounter of reader and text, a double and properly dialectical perspective on reading emerges; the reader reads the text, but the text also reads the reader.[5] The virtue of a transferential model would be to place intersubjectivity in the forefront, replacing the subject/object dualism with a more dialectical and temporal approach to the production of meaning.

David Bleich, whose work has followed similar lines, and whose critique of Holland's epistemology had a decisive influence on 5 Readers Reading (see Bleich 1978, pp. 115–16, n. 35), has suggested a way of saving subjectivity so as to make it intersubjectively useful by refocusing on the centrality of language as the mediating and objectifying agent. In his account of the 'subjective paradigm' (Subjective Criticism, 1978), all texts are 'symbolizations' formed in the reader's mind. The coherent and ordered response of critical discourse is a 're-symbolization' constrained not by an autonomous text or by individual self-consciousness but by the category of a shared intersubjective interest in knowledge. Truth and knowledge are the products of linguistic response. They are always already a function of interpretation which is validated not by reference to any universal or constant objective fact or cause, but by 'negotiation' which will lead to a collective decision by the members of a community about what will count as 'truth' and 'knowledge'. (This view recalls Fish's 'interpretive communities' but whereas for Fish, just as for semiotically oriented critics such as Culler, the concept of 'community' refers to a shared set of perceptual and interpretive strategies – a given construct already in place, by which the individual is produced and into which he is assimilated – Bleich's 'community' comes into being through a conscious process of negotiating individual choices and intentions.) Thus, in Bleich's theory, we 'objectify' experience by naming it and agreeing about the naming.

That the subjective paradigm, when put into practice, leads logically to objectivism and subverts its own theoretical foundations is indeed a major difficulty with Bleich's painstaking proposals.[6] But it is a difficulty well earned if it has served to reinsert the problematic of a mediating role played by 'language' rather than 'people' in a subjectivist model. Language, Bleich reminds us, is the act by which we transform an experience into an object of reflection. As the agent of a process of conceptualizing and predicating meaning, it occupies the space of contradiction and conflict – the difference – between subjectivity and objectivity.

Psychoanalysis and literary analysis

As in most traditional psychoanalytic criticism, Holland's informing premise is that the psychological meaning underlies all other meanings, and that some mode of psychoanalysis can teach literature and its readers what they don't know about their unconscious selves. But as I have indicated, any investigation of response in psychoanalytic terms will have to contend with the problematic nature of the grounds of knowledge adduced to that end. A psychoanalytic approach to the subject of reading finds itself entangled in a crux of queries converging on the question of the reading subject. Do psychoanalytic principles serve to reveal the buried contents of an author's mind and thereby teach us something about the creative process? Or do we invoke such principles to illuminate and interpret the nature of fictional characters? Alternatively, can we invoke the same principles to expound the mechanisms of interaction between readers and texts? Literary interpretation has resorted variously to the psychoanalytic conceptual framework in order to engage with each of these possibilities. Holland himself has sketched a history of interpretation which identifies three phases of psychoanalysis: 'a psychology first of the unconscious, second a psychology of the ego, and today, I believe, a psychology of the self' (1976, p. 223; see also 1980b). Binding these phases is the centring concern with 'human uniqueness' (p. 224) rather than the elusive nature of symbolic representation.

A shift of emphasis, however, might have yielded a rather different history. One possible direction is taken in Lionel Trilling's classic essay 'Freud and literature' (1961, first published 1951). Freud's discoveries, Trilling argued, are in many ways the culmination of the Romantic interest in the anti-rational dimensions of the human consciousness, and his systematic account of the human mind is the only one which 'in point of subtlety and complexity, of interest and tragic power deserves to stand beside the chaotic mass of psycho-logical insights which literature has accumulated through the centuries' (p. 34). But the positivistic application of this system in the elucidation, for instance, of authorial motives and predilections, has obscured Freud's more radical insights. The relevance of Freud's psychoanalysis for literary study is not, in Trilling's view, in the transmissibility of a *method* of interpretation (revealing the latent or concealed contents) but in the metapsychology underwriting that method. By showing how the unconscious mind organizes itself in 'figurative formations' – devices such as condensation, displacement and symbolization – Freud sketched a 'science of tropes' which 'naturalizes' poetry (p. 33), 'makes poetry indigenous to the constitution of the mind' (p. 52). On this point Trilling's reading of Freud anticipates Lacanian thought; and it is only a short step that leads from the overlap linking mind with figure to the entanglement of the science of poetry in the poetry of Freud's science.

An account, then, of the relationship between psychoanalysis and literary analysis centred on *rhetoric* rather than the individual *reader* would yield a somewhat different set of concerns from Holland's. Primarily one would be led to interrogate how *literally* and absolutely, or *literarily* and sceptically we espouse the psychoanalytic text. To be sure, the power of the Freudian mythology or language is such that we are all, in a sense, Freudians despite ourselves. The Freudian discourse has so naturalized itself within our speech and modes of thinking that foundational concepts such as ego, drive, defence, repression, and many others map a field of forces by which we verbally define our experience. But their precise epistemological and ontological status, and their scientific certifiability, remain elusive. As I suggest in the opening remarks to this chapter, recent commentary on the Freudian system has drawn attention to the extent to which its methods of interpretation are perplexed by a textuality into which analyst and analysand, dreamer and interpreter, are disconcertingly collapsed. Whether we regard these epistemological risks as a vicious and solipsistic short-circuiting or a benign and usable subjectivity will depend on our overall view of the hermeneutic procedure. Karl Kraus remarked acerbically that Freud's talking cure was the disease of which it purports to be the cure. But in Paul Ricoeur's honorific assessment of the Freudian discovery, it is precisely this straddling of a duplicity and doubleness which is perceived as the major philosophical breakthrough. Ricoeur situates Freud in company with Marx and Nietzsche as the founders of a pioneering hermeneutic 'school of suspicion' which demystifies the language of desire and the received lies of Cartesian consciousness. 'Beginning with them', he claims, 'understanding is hermeneutics; henceforward, to seek meaning is no longer to spell out the consciousness of meaning, but to *decipher its expressions*' (1970, p. 33); for they have created 'a mediate *science* of meaning, irreducible to the immediate consciousness of meaning' (1970, p. 34).

Evidently, the question which is the 'true' Freud cannot

even be posed in the wake of such demystification. Empirically, Freud himself continued to revise himself in the course of a long career, and his successors have privileged different margins, cruxes, or emphases within that colossal opus. Viennese Freuds are not identical with American Freuds or with French Freuds. As for literary Freuds, Harold Bloom may be taken for their spokesman when he claims that Freud is so 'strong' a writer (which is to say that his text both exemplifies and explores the limits of language with such reckless mastery and such a versatile willingness to take risks) that 'we read Freud not as we read Jung or Rank, Abraham or Ferenczi, but as we read Proust or Joyce, Valery or Rilke or Stevens' (1982, p. 92). The upshot of this turn is to situate psychoanalysis precariously within a very general orbit of reading and writing. Within this orbit, to read Freud's text as a literary text is to shift the perception of overlap between psychoanalysis and literature to an area of rhetoricity which complicates if not entirely displaces the question of what psychoanalysis can teach literature about its unconscious by its mirroring double: what can literature teach psychoanalysis about *its* repressed interiority, or, to quote Felman once again (p. 10), 'its *otherness-to-itself*, its unconscious'. But of course, without the centre or source of psychoanalytic precept and insight, the question could not even be asked. Even our interrogations of Freud remain Freudian.

6

The peripatetic reader: Wolfgang Iser and the aesthetics of reception

> Duke: And what's her history?
> Viola: A blank, my lord: she never told . . .
>
> (Shakespeare, *Twelfth Night*, II.v.110–11)

[handwritten annotation: aesthetics of literary reception of against aesthetics of literary production]

The turn to the reader, as a specifically native American phenomenon, comes in diverse guises, including the hospitable reception rendered by the American academy to the work of a German critic, Wolfgang Iser. For the Anglo-American reading public, Iser is the leading exponent of reception theory, whose two major works, *The Implied Reader: Patterns of Communication in Prose Fiction from Bunyan to Beckett* (1974) and *The Act of Reading: A Theory of Aesthetic Response* (1978), 'outsell' (so Stanley Fish reports in a devastating review (1981) to which I shall return) 'all other books on the prestigious list of the Johns Hopkins Press with the exception of *Grammatology*' (p. 2). Iser's name is associated with the school of *Rezeptionsästhetik* that has sprung up at the University of Konstanz in West Germany, whose focal interest, as its name indicates, is the aesthetics of literary reception. Within this framework, Iser's special concern is the reading process without which the aesthetics of reception cannot be described.

Unlike American reader-response criticism, German reception theory at Konstanz has developed as the cohesive and collective enterprise of a group of scholars who consciously share a critical platform, and who meet regularly to discuss and exchange ideas. One of their chief spokesmen is Hans Robert Jauss (1982), whose project aims to develop a new mode of literary history based not on a simple positivistic acceptance of received tradition but rather on an investigation of the literary reception of canonical works, and on the ways in which the experience of the literary work by its readers mediates the relationship of past and present.

The label *Rezeptionsästhetik* by which the methodology of the Konstanz school is usually identified is a word which does not lend itself to exact translation into English. One problem within the general shift of concern from text-and-author to text-and-reader is the precise distinction between the concepts of *Rezeption* and *Wirkung*; *Wirkung* 'comprises both effect and response, without the psychological connotations of the English word "response"' (Iser, 1978, p. ix n.). The assumption here is that a theory of response 'has its roots in the text' whereas a theory of reception 'arises from a history of readers' judgments' (p. x) so that *Rezeptionsästhetik* emphasizes audience reception whereas *Wirkungsästhetik* emphasizes the potential effect of the text, and concentrates on the interaction between reader and text. 'Effects and responses are properties neither of the text nor of the reader', Iser claims; 'the text represents a potential effect that is realized in the reading process' (p. ix). This realization is the scene of operations in which Iser is interested and of which he attempts to provide a total theoretical account.

Unlike the collaborative endeavour at Konstanz, the broad label of 'reader-response' criticism, under which different American critical persuasions shelter, has been applied '*ex post facto*', as Robert C. Holub remarks in his recent introduction to reception theory, 'to a number of writers who have very little contact with or influence on one another'. Indeed, Holub adds, 'if reader-response criticism has become a critical force, as some would maintain, it is by virtue of the ingenuity of labeling rather than any commonalty of effort' (1984, pp. xii–xiii). The partial truth of this observation in no way invalidates Wolfgang Iser's right to the title of the 'total' or compleat reader-response critic.

In contrast to the self-revising structure of American reader-response criticism, Iser's work takes the form of a consistent and undeviating elaboration of his seminal ideas which first appeared in 'Die Appellstruktur der Texte' in 1970, translated into English as 'Indeterminacy and the reader's response to prose fiction' (1971). *The Implied Reader* (1974) is a collection of essays on prose fiction from Bunyan to Beckett in which ten of the eleven chapters are the application of the phenomenological theory of reading, harking back to the 1970 essay, expounded in the eleventh. *The Act of Reading* (1978) is, in effect, a laborious working out of the same ideas, amplified by a mass of diverse theoretical speculation (such as speech–act theory, Gestalt psychology, narrative theory, communication theory, etc.) yoked onto the same basic phenomenological model.[1] The short essay 'Interaction between text and reader' in Suleiman's collection (1980) is actually a cento of excerpts from *The Act of Reading* and can serve as an abridged introduction to Iser's theory. My own resumé draws on *The Act of Reading*, which provides the fullest account.

But before addressing myself to this account and its philosophical underpinnings in the work of Roman Ingarden, let me introduce another related school of thought – the Geneva school of consciousness[2] – represented here by Georges Poulet's account (1969) of the phenomenology of reading as a reciprocal 'transparency of minds'.

Georges Poulet and the phenomenology of reading

It should by now be abundantly clear that the single most recalcitrant feature of theories of reading is the difficulty of theorizing the relationship of reader to text or of subject to object. The question of authority for literary meaning remains the bone of contention because theories of reading, as Jonathan Culler has observed, 'demonstrate the impossibility of establishing well-grounded distinctions between fact and interpretation, between what can be read in the text and what is read into it' (1982, p. 75). The phenomenological approach to which we turn in this chapter promises to account for the convergence or merging of subject and object more elegantly than most because it encompasses the dualism of reader and text, of act and structure in a single concept, the concept of intentionality.

According to phenomenological accounts, all consciousness is consciousness of something. Although we cannot be certain of the independent 'objective' existence of things, we can be certain of their presence as things intended by consciousness. Intentionality here does not mean desire, or what the author meant to say, but denotes the structure of an act by which the subject imagines, or conceptualizes, or is conscious of an object, thereby bringing the object into being; but the intuition of the object simultaneously constitutes the subject as a vessel of consciousness. The subject is thus (in intending the object) paradoxically the origin of all meaning but is also the effect of consciousness. In such a structure the traditional subject/object dichotomy disintegrates.

'The extraordinary fact in the case of a book is the falling away of the barriers between you and it. You are inside it; it is inside you; there is no longer either outside or inside.' This is the initial phenomenon observed in Georges Poulet's description (1969, p. 54) of the text–reader relationship. Until an act of human intervention takes place to release it from its mute materiality, the book is an inert object. It should be noted here that for Poulet, who is not at all interested in a book's formal features, the book or text must be rigorously distinguished from the 'work'. A book requires a reading consciousness for its realization as a work. Upon being read, the 'object' disappears into a new existence in the reader's 'innermost self' where its material reality ceases to exist and it becomes a mental entity (image, idea, word), an intention or 'subjectified' object which is the transparent consciousness of another. Within the reader the work lives its own life; 'in a certain sense, it thinks itself, and it even gives itself a meaning within me' (p. 59). This annexation of the reader's consciousness does not mean that he is deprived of consciousness, but that his consciousness is identified with another's. As soon as a book has entered the shelter of the reader's innermost self and the reader begins to play host to this other consciousness, an astonishing intimacy develops in which the barriers between subject and object fall away. The semi-mystical experience is best expressed in Poulet's own words:

This is the remarkable transformation wrought in me

through the act of reading. Not only does it cause the physical objects around me to disappear, including the very book I am reading, but it replaces those external objects with a congeries of mental objects in close *rapport* with my own consciousness. And yet the very intimacy in which I now live with my objects is going to present me with new problems. The most curious of these is the following: I am someone who happens to have as objects of his own thought, thoughts which are part of a book I am reading, and which are therefore the cogitations of another. They are the thoughts of another, and yet it is I who am their subject. The situation is even more astonishing than the one noted above. I am thinking the thoughts of another. Of course, there would be no cause for astonishment if I were thinking it as the thought of another. But I think it as my very own. . . . Because of the strange invasion of my person by the thoughts of another, I am a self who is granted the experience of thinking thoughts foreign to him. I am the subject of thoughts other than my own. My consciousness behaves as though it were the consciousness of another. . . . Whatever I think is part of *my* mental world. And yet here I am thinking a thought which manifestly belongs to another mental world, which is being thought in me just as though I did not exist. . . . Whenever I read, I mentally pronounce an *I*, and yet the *I* which I pronounce is not myself . . . for as soon as something is presented as *thought*, there has to be a thinking subject with whom, at least for the time being, I identify, forgetting myself, alienated from myself.

(pp. 55–6)

From this description it may appear that the thinking being who has displaced the reader's consciousness is the author. But Poulet adds a disclaimer. The subject that presides over the work can exist only in the work, and whatever connection the work may have to the author's existence is external to the merging of consciousness that occurs during reading. 'The subject who is revealed to me through my reading of it is not the author'. To be sure, biographical, textual, and general critical information is indispensable but 'this knowledge does not coincide with the internal knowledge of the work'. At the moment of reading 'what matters to me is to live, from the inside, in a certain identity with the work and the work alone' (p. 58). This work, constituted by the animating intention of the reader, 'becomes (at the expense of the reader whose own life it suspends) a sort of human being . . . a mind conscious of itself and constituting itself in me as the subject of its own objects' (p. 59).

It is apparent that the appropriation of consciousness Poulet describes is the opposite, say, of Holland's replication of identity. For the reader, given over entirely to his book, the active intending of a meaning is an absorption which effaces rather than replicates personal identity. 'I am a consciousness astonished by an existence which is not mine, but which I experience as though it were mine' (p. 60). Neither author nor reader, in Poulet's account, is master of the intended object of consciousness.

Roman Ingarden and the concretization of the object

If the key phenomenon in Poulet's account of the way in which literature realizes itself in the reader is a moment of self-surrender and passive reception, in Iser's account the reader actively participates in the assemblage of literary meaning. The philosophical influence behind Iser is also phenomenology; more specifically, it is the application of Husserl's theories by his disciple and friend, the Polish philosopher Roman Ingarden (1973), to literary works.

Central to Ingarden's philosophy is a distinction between the ontological status of the work of art, and the epistemological status of the cognitive activities by which the reader 'concretizes' the work. For Ingarden the work is a purely intentional object which does not have a full existence without the participation of consciousness, yet does not depend entirely on a subject for its existence. Ingarden distinguishes between two kinds of objects, 'autonomous' or determinate, and 'ontically heteronomous' objects. Autonomous objects have immanent properties, whilst heteronomous objects are characterized by a combination of immanent or inherent properties, and properties attributed to them by consciousness. Without the operations of a subject–object relationship, they do not have a full existence.

The literary work of art, according to Ingarden, presents the perfect case of an ontically heteronomous formation whose mode of existence exemplifies a purely intentional object – neither ideal nor real, but one which requires an act of concretization or realization by a reader. Ingarden, however, insists on maintaining a distinction between the object's independent existence, on the one hand, and its concretizations in the act of reading, on the other. In his account, the heteronomous object consists of several determinate layers or strata. First there is a layer of phonetic formations or sound configurations; then a layer of syntactic and semantic units (whether words, sentences or larger units) arising from the first strata; out of these a layer of schematized objects (the characters, setting, etc.) is constituted; finally we have a layer of represented objects (the author's world), which is the product and culmination of the other three layers. The totality of these strata constitutes a skeletal polyphonic harmony or schematized structure whose 'indeterminate places' must be completed by the reader.

This was the ontological outline, borrowed from Ingarden, underlying Wellek's description of the mode of existence of the literary object (see p. 59). For the New Critic, Ingarden's theory provided the licence for promoting an 'intrinsic' approach to the artwork, whereas for Iser the same emphasis on the heteronomous object promotes a reader-response criticism which, however, retains a strongly formalist slant. The common source probably explains to a certain extent the formalistic, classicist and totalizing residue of Iser's interpretations despite his anti-formalist polemicizing.

Because perception construes a complete object from a limited number of perceived properties, the objects represented in a literary work exhibit (in contrast to autonomous objects) an infinite number of points of indeterminacy or gaps which must be filled or completed by a reading consciousness. The work of reading is thus a creative process of 'concretization'; it bridges the gaps in the structure and fills out the schematized aspects of the text, determining the places of indeterminacy and actualizing the potential of the schemata. This activity, although governed by the schematized aspects, draws on the reader's personal experience, and requires both skill and imagination; and since no two readers are identical, no two concretizations will be identical, even when they are the work of the same reader. While the work itself is invariable and stable, the number of possible concretizations is unlimited and will differ from reader to reader. Furthermore, no single concretization will exhaust the possibilities contained in the virtual work or will be identical with it.

What is problematic in Ingarden's account, and remains a problem in Iser's appropriation of Ingarden's model, is the determinable status he attributes to the skeletal schemata which constitute the virtual structure of the work. As Ingarden would have it, the work is a purely intentional object, yet it is not entirely dependent on the subject for its existence. The entire system thus depends on the double identity of the literary work's objective status and its subjective realization in the reading process. But what remains unclear is why perception of the objective structure is immune to infinite indeterminacy, and is not itself a concretization. In other words, the distinction Ingarden wishes to establish between the ontological status of literary objects and the epistemological status of cognitive activities is difficult to maintain.[3] This very difficulty haunts Iser's model too.

Wolfgang Iser: gaps, blanks and indeterminacies

Central to Iser's intuition is the view that reading consists of an *interaction* between the structure of the literary work and its recipient. His model, therefore, presents three interrelated aspects of the reading process: there is the *text* with its supposed schemata or layers of determination and the concomitant places of indeterminacy, constituting a potential for the production of meaning; there is the *reader's processing* of the text – his construction or concretization of a cohesive aesthetic object by means of a synthesizing or consistency-building activity; and finally there are the *conditions* that give rise to and govern *the text–reader interaction*. Here, in Iser's words, is a compact description of the shape of the model:

the literary work has two poles, which we might call the artistic and the aesthetic: the artistic pole is the author's text and the aesthetic is the realization accomplished by the reader. In view of this polarity, it is clear that the work itself cannot be identical with the text or with the concretization, but must be situated somewhere between the two. It must inevitably be virtual in character, as it cannot be reduced to the reality of the text or to the subjectivity of the reader, and it is from this virtuality that it derives its dynamism. As the reader passes through the various perspectives offered by the text and relates the different views and patterns to one another he sets the work in motion, and so sets himself in motion too.

(1978, p. 21)

The virtue of this model, as Iser sees it, is that it avoids identifying the aesthetic object either with an objective self-sufficient text (the artistic pole) or with the subjective experience of an individual reader (the aesthetic pole). Iser insists that the literary text does not point to a referential reality (as does a 'document') but represents a pattern, 'a structured indicator to guide the imagination of the reader' (p. 9). This set of instructions, however, is incomplete, full of 'gaps' or 'blanks' or 'indeterminacies' which must be filled by the reader, both according to his disposition and to the perspectives offered by the text. Meaning is not directly accessible or even present in any way either in the reader or in the textual object, but is something that emerges (a product or assemblage) in the process of interaction between the two poles. The meaning, Iser claims, 'can only be grasped as an image. The image provides the filling for what the textual pattern structures but leaves out' (p. 9). The reader is free to fill in the blanks but is at the same time constrained by the patterns supplied in the text; the text proposes, or instructs, and the reader disposes, or constructs. 'Imagistic' in character, meaning is dependent upon the reader's imagination; it is to be found neither in the words printed on the page nor outside the book (i.e. referentially) but

must clearly be the product of an interaction between the textual signals and the reader's acts of comprehension. . . . As text and reader thus merge into a single situation, the division between subject and object no longer applies, and it therefore follows that meaning is no longer an object to be defined, but is an effect to be experienced.

(pp. 9–10)

On this point Iser seems to be closer to Poulet's than to Ingarden's view, for Ingarden implies that the message is transmitted in a 'one-way incline from text to reader' whereas in Iser's view literary communication is a 'two-way relationship' (p. 173) insofar as the reader's 'reception' of the 'message' of a literary work means that he is 'composing' it; 'the meaning of a literary text', Iser insists, 'is not a definable entity but, if anything, a dynamic happening' (p. 22). But unlike Poulet, Iser's initial premise insists on the non-coincidence of reader and text.

Nevertheless, this remains a slippery point because, with regard to the identity of the reader, Iser manages to straddle two sides of a fence, one text-centred and hypothetical, the other reader-centred and empirical. His term, the Implied Reader, is evidently a counterpart to Wayne C. Booth's (1961) Implied Author, and is, on the one hand, firmly rooted in the text. The Implied Reader

> embodies all those predispositions necessary for a literary work to exercise its effect – predispositions laid down, not by an empirical outside reality, but by the text itself. Consequently, the implied reader as a concept has his roots firmly planted in the structure of the text; he is a construct and in no way to be identified with any real reader.

(p. 34)

But on the other hand, the textual construct can only be construed by a real reader, so that the concept of an Implied Reader has two basic and interrelated aspects, textual and empirical: 'the concept of the implied reader designates a network of response-inviting structures, which impel the reader to grasp the text' (p. 34). This duality of actual reader and Implied Reader was adumbrated in Iser's earlier study (1974) in which the Implied Reader is the entity or persona which 'incorporates both the prestructuring of the potential meaning by the text, and the reader's actualization of this potential through the reading process' (p. xii).

By using this double-barrelled definition, Iser manages both to distinguish and divide and at the same time to join 'the reader's role as a textual structure, and the reader's role as a structured act' (1978, p. 35). The sophistication of this dialectical manoeuvring, however, is achieved at the cost of blurring the distinction which Iser assumes throughout his work between the conceptualized phenomenological reader and empirical or historical readers. It is a definition which also enables him to skirt the obstinate question of which side of the partnership wields authority for the production of literary meaning. Perhaps that is why the concept of the Implied Reader plays a very reticent role in the elaboration of the model, and especially in the account of the conditions governing the text–reader interaction.

The text itself, according to Iser, can never be grasped as a whole – 'only as a series of changing viewpoints, each one restricted in itself and so necessitating further perspectives. This is the process by which the reader "realizes" an overall situation' (p. 68). The reader's acts of comprehension are structured by his attempts to build up a consistent view of the textual segments as he moves between the shifting perspectives of the text. Inspired by eighteenth-century novelists, Iser likens the reader's construction of Gestalten to

> a traveler in a stagecoach who has to make the often difficult journey through the novel, gazing out from his moving viewpoint. Naturally, he combines all that he sees within his memory and establishes a pattern of consistency, the nature and reliability of which will depend partly on the degree of attention he has paid during each phase of the journey. At no time, however, can he have a total view of that journey.
> (p. 16)

The metaphor of a journey is explored in Iser's outline of a governing structure of comprehension which he calls foreground-and-background, or theme-and-horizon. A narrative text, for instance, is composed of a variety of perspectives between which the reader's wandering viewpoint moves. (In most narratives there are four main perspectives: 'that of the narrator, that of the characters, that of the plot, and that marked out for the reader' (p. 96).) As the reader's viewpoint travels between segments his focus on a perspective will form a theme (or foreground) in relation to which the rest are horizon (or background) – until she/he moves on, and the theme of a moment ago will in turn become horizon. The journey through perspectives and shifting themes and horizons is accomplished by virtue of the reader's incessant acts of ideation, as she/he organizes segments and construes the connection between them, always preoccupied by gap-filling activities that ultimately produce the synthesis we think of as comprehension or meaning.

What then are the conditions of this experience or interaction? The interaction is governed by the ubiquitous presupposition that there is no immaculate perception and that the meeting place of the artistic and aesthetic poles is a constitutive absence which Iser variously names a blank or gap or indeterminacy. Drawing on psychoanalytic research into interpersonal perception and communication, Iser quotes R.D. Laing on the insurmountable barriers which confine the relationship of self and other: '*your experience of me is invisible to me and my experience of you is invisible to you.* I cannot experience your experience. You cannot experience my experience. We are both invisible men. All men are invisible to one another. Experience is man's invisibility to man' (p. 165). This invisibility (Laing calls it a 'no-thing') structures interpersonal experience in which contact depends on filling in the absent or invisible by an act of interpretation, and this interpretation constitutes the process of interaction. Iser believes (on insufficient grounds, I think, and against the pathos of Laing's text) that in personal face-to-face relationships this dyadic psychological model of human interaction has a regulative context, whereas in a text–reader relationship there is no face-to-face situation. The text does not talk back to correct one's misinterpretations; it cannot adapt, assert, defend itself or supplement its fragmented codes. It is, as Iser says, characterized by a lack of ascertainability or of defined intention. There is thus a fundamental asymmetry between text and reader. The text is full of gaps or blanks; and – as in a social situation, so too in the textual situation – the gaps (the unspoken dialogue or the unwritten text) are that which induces communication. Underlying the process of interaction is 'an indeterminate, constitutive blank . . . which is continually bombarded with projections' (p. 167), so that it is 'the very lack of ascertainability and defined intention that brings about the text–reader interaction' (p. 166).

Since the gaps in a text can be filled in many different ways every text is potentially capable of many different realizations and no reading can exhaust the text's full potential which is always infinitely richer than any of its realizations. What transforms the text into an experience for the reader is a process of ideation (the formation of ideas in the mind) regulated by an active interweaving of anticipation and retrospection by which we gather – as in real life – the impressions that result in something we call experience. For no two readers will the experience be identical: 'two people gazing at the night sky may both be looking at the same collection of stars, but one will see the image of a plough, and the other will make out a dipper. The "stars" in a literary text are fixed; the lines that join them are variable' (1974, p. 282).

There is also a historical dimension to Iser's theory of the literary text that moves counter to his prevalent anti-referential bias. Literary texts in general, Iser believes, constitute a reaction to contemporary situations, bringing attention to problems that are conditioned though not resolved by contemporary norms. This is to say that prior to the text–reader interaction there was an interaction between the author and the social and historical norms of his environment. Literary texts are thus acts of communication whose purpose is to reformulate existing thought-systems in order to bring about 'the imaginary correction of deficient realities' (p. 85). The systems of perspectives in the novel or story refer the reader to social or historical or cultural and aesthetic aspects of reality and invite him to scrutinize them in a new combination. This scrutiny is an experience which the reader undergoes. In other words, the reader's interaction with the text in the way described (theme-and-horizon structured by blanks) leads not only to the structuring of a configuration in his imagination (the act of ideation and comprehension) but also to a discovery and a formulation of 'alien' thoughts which invade our consciousness, leading us to 'discover an inner world of which we had hitherto not been conscious' (p. 158). Reading is thus an active process of becoming conscious of otherness, as it brings about a questioning and probing of the validity of received norms and systems. In brief, it is an event of personal and social significance, an expansion of the self.

The attractiveness of Iser's theory apparently lies in his attempt to accommodate as broad a spectrum of theoretical speculation as possible, and to integrate it all within a total theory of reading which will do justice to every component in the act of communication: author, text, reader, the world, the process of reception, the phenomenology of perception and reading, the dynamic nature of comprehension – all these are apparently brought together and integrated in the one model of aesthetic response.

The dyadic shape of the theory is both its strength and its weakness. On the one hand we have a determinate textual structure which guides and instructs the reader's response. On the other hand, the life of the text depends entirely on the interpretation. This doubleness is vital for establishing the interactive text–reader relationship, whilst managing to avoid the question of interpretive authority. The 'relative indeterminacy' of the text, the presence of gaps and blanks which must be filled by an interpreting subject, privileges the participation and creative imagination of the reader who co-authors the literary work. But this seemingly fair distribution of authority between two centres is, as Iser's critics have pointed out, difficult to maintain. It is possible to argue that from the perspective of the artistic pole, everything depends ultimately on the author's stable text which supplies all that the interpreter requires; but viewed from the perspective of the aesthetic pole the author's text is deprived of all authority, and any textual 'fact' such as a blank will be the product of a certain reading strategy, so that all is supplied by the reader. The compromise formation whereby the text instructs and the reader constructs breaks down under critical scrutiny.

In other words, I am proposing that Iser's critical text becomes the itinerary for a wandering viewpoint which fails to reach a destination in a metacritical landscape whose co-ordinates (object/subject, text/reader, artistic/aesthetic) disorient the stability of the discursive map. Without the fixed points of the compass the journey is unthinkable; the attempt to fix them is to discover their variability and instability. Without our conceptualizing map we cannot proceed; to proceed, however, is to discover the unreliability of the co-ordinates which provide, not safe conduct, but entry into a labyrinth.

The indeterminacy of reader-response criticism

I should like to conclude this survey of Iser's project by restaging the somewhat rancorous debate between Stanley Fish and Wolfgang Iser that took place in the pages of *Diacritics* some five years ago. The debate, at whose centre stands the vexed issue of (in)determinacy, touches on some of the central problems of reader-response criticism at large.

In his provocative review of *The Act of Reading*, 'Why no one's afraid of Wolfgang Iser' (1981), Fish notes what he considers to be a curious feature of the reception of Iser in American academic circles: 'he is influential without being controversial, and at a moment when everyone is choosing up sides, he seems to be on no side at all or (it amounts to the same thing) on every side at once' (p. 2). This effect of appeasement and reconciliation is due to the fact that Iser's is a 'capacious and liberal theory' that seems particularly well suited to the 'pluralistic' proclivities of a certain stream in contemporary criticism whose tendency is 'to steer a middle way between the poles of objectivity and subjectivity' (p. 3). This brand of pluralism contends that while a text is open to more than one reading, it is not open to any or all readings; 'plurality is not an infinity' (p. 4). Pluralist practice, therefore, 'requires . . . a theory that can accommodate the diversity of interpretation and yet at the same time identify the constraints that prevent interpretation from being arbitrary' (p. 4). Iser's theory, Fish argues, meets this requirement by performing acts of accommodation all along the line, in multiple concessions to both sides of traditional oppositions such as author/reader, literature/life, self/other, subjectivity/objectivity, ontology/epistemology, etc. 'And yet, in the end it falls apart, and it falls apart because the distinction on which it finally depends – the distinction between the determinate and the indeterminate – will not hold' (p. 6).

What is at stake in this debate is not only the indeterminacy of meaning but the indeterminacy of the grounding facts prior to meaning. It will be recalled that for Stanley Fish 'the brute-fact' status of the text cannot be taken for granted. The seemingly objective and autonomous facts embedded in the text are not given, but are the result of our perceptual strategies or reading acts. The category of the 'given' is always already the interpretation of an indeterminacy so that 'the determinacies or textual segments, the indeterminacies or gaps, and the adventures of the reader's "wandering viewpoint" – will be the products of an interpretive strategy that demands them' (p. 7). This is not to say that Fish denies the possibility of giving an account of a literary text which will make a distinction between what is supplied by the text and what by the reader; only that such a procedure conceals a false assumption which Fish would like to correct: 'the distinction itself is an assumption which, when it informs an act of literary description, will *produce* the phenomena it purports to describe' (p. 7). What Fish engages, in other words, is the grounding presupposition of Iser's theory that *something* is determinately given. For Fish, nothing is given, and the reader supplies '*everything*: the stars in a literary text are not fixed; they are just as variable as the lines that join them' (p. 7). Put another way, 'perception is never innocent of assumptions, and the assumptions within which it occurs will be responsible for the contours of what is perceived' (p. 8).

Given Fish's alternative set of assumptions, the determinacy/ indeterminacy opposition loses its force. From Fish's meta-critical perspective, it would make just as much sense to say that everything is determinate as to say that everything is indeterminate, for these categories are irrelevant when there is no way for a reader to place himself beyond the assumptions of a system of intelligibility. And without the possibility of making the crucial distinction between determinate and indeterminate, the cohesive centre of Iser's entire system disappears.

Iser's rejoinder ('Talk like whales', 1981) is to the effect that the process of hermeneutics simply short-circuits into monistic solipsism ('whenever I read Professor Fish I keep rubbing my eyes in order to make sure that I am not reading Bishop

Berkeley') if we fuse 'interpretation and that which is to be interpreted into an indistinguishable whole' (p. 84). Iser agrees that there is no unmediated given but resists Fish's monism on the grounds that 'interpretation would be useless if it were not meant to open access to something we encounter' (p. 84). The 'something' which 'exists prior to interpretation, acts as a constraint on interpretation . . . and thus contributes to a hermeneutical process, the result of which is both a mediated given and a reshuffling of the initial assumptions' (p. 84). Iser also clarifies that the given is not identical with the determinate but prior to it. Determinacy is the result of interpreting the given.

> Professor Fish's confusion is caused by the fact that he has telescoped three ideas into two. I draw a distinction between the given, the determinate, and the indeterminate. I maintain that the literary world differs from the real world because it is only accessible to the imagination, whereas the real world is also accessible to the senses and exists outside any description of it. The words of a text are given, the interpretation of the words is determinate, and the gaps between given elements and/or interpretations are the indeterminacies. The real world is given, our interpretation of the world is determinate, the gaps between given elements and/or our interpretations are the indeterminacies. The difference is that with the literary text, it is the interpretation of the words that produces the literary world – i.e. its real-ness, unlike that of the outside world, is not given.
>
> (p. 83)

This reply sharply focuses the difference between Iser's dualism and Fish's monism but seems to miss or evade the force of Fish's real objection which is that the 'given' cannot be perceived as 'given' (let alone meaningful) unless we endow it with the status of 'given-ness' by an act of interpretation. Fish is not confused at all about the distinctions – he simply puts them in doubt. To identify anything as given is to operate from within the constraints of an ideology or an assumption already in place. Iser resists the challenge to question the assumptions behind the assumptions by a repetition of his old positions. But he could also have pressed the point that Fish's line of argument (nothing is given) leads into what may prove to be an ultimately empty or trivial abyss of infinite regress, with little consequence regarding the activity of reading: without a trigger ('something' to be interpreted) no act of interpretation can take place.

Either way it seems that the dispute leads not to a settlement but to a highlighting of the two basic and basically irreconcilable positions between which reader-response criticism moves, and which are frequently identified with the terms objectivity and subjectivity.

In conclusion: reading reading

'Indeterminacy' is a word with bad vibes. It evokes a
picture of the critic as Hamlet, 'sicklied o'er with the
pale cast of thought'.

(Geoffrey H. Hartman, *Criticism in the Wilderness*)

One immediate conclusion that suggests itself from the
foregoing survey of reader-response criticisms is the existence
of an insurmountable rift between theory and practice. As we
have seen, theories of reader-response seek to revise the aims
and methods of literary study not only by reminding us that
the reader is an active participant in the production of
meaning, but also by impersonating or characterizing, in some
form or other, a reader who assumes dominance or authority
over a text. In prosecuting the logic of the reader's appropriation
of and mastery over the text, the reader-response critic shifts
the scene of operations from a timeless, objective, self-sufficient
text to a reader's mind, and puts in question the text's
autonomous existence, thereby also putting in question our
orthodox assumptions about the distance or difference between
text and reader.[1] It would seem, therefore, that theoretically
the distinction between the objective and the subjective,
between the literary fact (or the author's text) and the
interpretive act (or the reader's construction) cannot be
maintained. In practice, however, the distinction always
returns; it is always being made so that acts of interpretation
can continue to be produced. Reader-response criticisms are at
once generated and undone by this unresolved tension.

The experience of reader-response criticism teaches us that
the distinction hasn't a theoretical leg to stand on – we are

always in a context of interpretation – but it also teaches us that such distinctions are always being made in practice. 'We employ [them] all the time', says Jonathan Culler, 'because our stories [of reading] require them, but they are variable and ungrounded concepts' (1982, p. 77).

Is a resolution of this impasse imaginable? On the evidence of the attempts of reader-response criticisms to outline a total theory of reading – and Iser's project is a particularly striking instance – the answer is no.

My readings of reader-response criticisms suggest that inconclusiveness is intrinsic to these projects. This survey has explored the various ways in which they situate themselves in relation to two opposing demands regarding the question of literary meaning: one refers to the authority of an author's creation or word for the institution of an objective criticism, the other to the authority of a reader's recreation or response, for the institution of a subjective criticism. The most extreme statement of the first position is widely associated with the name of E.D. Hirsch and the view that 'hermeneutics must stress a reconstruction of the author's aims and attitudes in order to evolve guides and norms for construing the meanings of his text'.[2] The second, opposing position is well represented both by Stanley Fish's argument that the reader's cognitive activities supply everything – we 'write' the texts we read – and by Norman Holland's psychoanalytic argument that all reading replicates the reader. Somewhere in between stands Wolfgang Iser's desire to synthesize the two poles, or, alternatively, Jonathan Culler's recent insistence on the impossibility of such a synthesis.

> For the reader the work is not partially created but, on the one hand already complete and inexhaustible – one can read and reread without ever grasping completely what has already been made – and on the other hand, still to be created in the process of reading, without which it is only black marks on paper. The attempt to produce compromise formulations fails to capture this essential, divided quality of reading.
>
> (1982, p. 76)

In his critique of reader-response criticisms, Culler argues persuasively that the irreducible dichotomy of text and reader, object and subject, simply refuses to go away. Theoretical models which aspire to monism are systematically subverted by a lingering practical duality. Reader-response criticisms are thus both generated and destroyed in the dialectical interplay between the monism of theory and the dualism of practice.

If there is no escape from this bind, no conclusive resolution or master theory to settle the struggle between textual constraints and readers' experiences and histories; and if it is indeed an essential structural feature of the situation of reading, then at least the response to the bind (or should we now perceive it as an inescapable bond?) must hope to assume the dimensions of a rigorous responsibility[3] – by which I mean a reader's perpetual openness to whatever is 'counter, original, spare, strange' (G. M. Hopkins) in texts as well as in interpretations. Some such stance, as I see it, characterizes the overwhelming post-structuralist concern with the problematic of *reading*, not as a mastery or appropriation but as a patient dialogue or interrogation.

Although it becomes clear that the primacy of the reader as the founding term for a critical theory or practice is as vulnerable as earlier attempts to master and close the text, what the study of these explorations of reader-response nevertheless usefully yields is a sharpened awareness of what, and how much, is at stake in the act of reading. This awareness has infiltrated our consciousness so deeply that the reader can no longer be ignored, even when the pendulum swing of literary trends – and I have in mind the impact of deconstruction in particular – has taken us back to a new respect for the text's integrity and impenetrability. The various stories of reading beyond reader-response criticism (beyond, that is, the sustained efforts of the above projects to think their way through and around the subject/object dichotomy) are also beyond the scope of this introduction;[4] I shall therefore confine myself, by means of a handful of quotations, to the briefest thumbnail sketch of the development that I have found the most compelling.

From the perspective of a scrupulous linguistic scepticism, the late Paul de Man's closest of close readings demonstrate the view that 'the impossibility of reading should not be taken too lightly' because rhetoric puts 'an insurmountable obstacle in the way of any reading or understanding' (1979, pp. 245, 131) of both the literary and the critical text. It is in the realm of rhetoricity that author and reader meet, and what is there produced is not a reading that belongs to either reader or text, but is an 'allegory'.

> The reading is not 'our' reading, since it uses only the linguistic elements provided by the text itself; the distinction between author and reader is one of the false distinctions that reading makes evident. The deconstruction is not something we have added to the text but it constituted the text in the first place. A literary text simultaneously asserts and denies the authority of its own rhetorical mode, and by reading the text as we did we were only trying to come closer to being as rigorous a reader as the author had to be in order to write the sentence in the first place.
>
> (p. 17)

In a similar mode, J. Hillis Miller's deconstructive reading strategies tease out the moments of what he calls a text's 'unreadability', a notion that 'names the discomfort of [a] perpetual lack of closure'.

> Unreadability is the generation by the text itself of a desire for the possession of the *logos*, while at the same time the text itself frustrates this desire, in a torsion of undecidability which is intrinsic to language.
>
> (1980, p. 113)

For Miller, the reader can never hope to dominate a text or its meaning; she/he can only perform the roles inscribed or dramatized in the text's aporetic doubleness.

For Geoffrey Hartman, always a very reticent theoretician, reader and text are joined in a bond of 'troth rather than truth' (1981, p. 137), a dialogue or language exchange that will 'save the text by continuing it in our consciousness' (1980, p. 268). Both objective and subjective criticism, Hartman argues, 'ignore equally the resistance of art to the meanings it provokes'. To name the experience of this resistance he proposes the notion of 'indeterminacy' or 'negative hermeneutics'.

As a guiding concept, indeterminacy does not merely *delay* the determination of meaning, that is, suspend premature judgements and allow greater thoughtfulness. The delay is not heuristic alone, a device to slow the act of reading till we appreciate (I could think here of Stanley Fish) its complexity. The delay is intrinsic: from a certain point of view, it is thoughtfulness itself, Keats's 'negative capability', a labor that aims not to overcome the negative or indeterminate but to stay within it as long as it is necessary.

(1980, 269–70)

Indeterminacy invites a resistance to closure and an insistence on greater reflection and self-reflection – not as a methodology but as a 'speculative instrument' (Richards) in the service of reading.

I invoke Hartman here, as I did in my introduction, as the spokesman for my own understanding of the destinies of reading beyond reader-response criticism. Hence my last section-heading – reading reading – with its deliberate tension between identity and difference, noun and verb, primary and secondary; and its innuendoes of mirroring, repetition, recursion, reflexivity, analysis terminable and interminable. In turning to itself, reading also returns to the text. Hartman's meticulous respect for the text, however, never forgets (but also never prescribes) 'how much responsibility is on the respondent, on the interpreter. Dialogue itself is at stake' (1981, p. 134).

Dialogue I here take to be a trope for reading that stands in opposition to the authority of monological discourse, whether the text's or the reader's. Neither as self-abnegation, nor as 'an infinite incantation of our selves' (Wallace Stevens), reading continues, ever more closely and patiently, because, as de Man put it (1983, p. 32), the 'dialogue between work and interpreter is endless'.

Notes

Introduction

1 Cary Nelson ('Reading criticism' (1976) and 'The psychology of criticism' (1978)) explores the view that 'part of the psychology of criticism is the very tendency to deny that its psychology exists' (1978, p. 46).

2 Tompkins's narrative, which (mysteriously) omits Richards and (less mysteriously) deconstruction, is governed by the pragmaticist thesis that 'discourse is responsible for reality', and that the 'net result of this epistemological revolution is to repoliticize literature and literary criticism' and to restore their 'ability to influence human behaviour in a direct and practical manner' (p. xxv).

Another useful general survey can be found in the first two chapters of Stephen Mailloux's *Interpretive Conventions: The Reader in the Study of American Fiction* (1982).

From a somewhat different and more rhetorically sophisticated perspective, Jonathan Culler, in his post-structuralist phase (*On Deconstruction: Theory and Criticism After Structuralism* (1982) pp. 64–83), reviews several 'Stories of reading' to argue that theories seeking to ground literary meaning in the experience of the reader strain towards a monism that is undercut by the residual difference and dualism of reader and text, subject and object. This view corresponds in certain ways to my own version of the prototypical story of reading.

William Ray's *Literary Meaning: From Phenomenology to Deconstruction* (1984) is an excellent advanced introduction to the contemporary critical scene, and includes critiques of the main reader-response proponents.

3 Although the multiplication of reader-response criticisms, and the attention they have commanded, is a recent phenomenon, numerous critics in the past have written about the reader. Since I do not attempt an encyclopaedic survey, the list of omissions is embarrassingly long. I would like, therefore, to draw brief attention here to two critics whose valuable and interesting contributions have been excluded from the categories of this survey.

Of particular historical and pragmatic interest is the work of Louise M. Rosenblatt which bridges the era of Richards and the contemporary resurgence of interest in the reader. *Literature as Exploration* (1937) undertook to demonstrate, in a Ricardian spirit, 'how intimately the materials of human relations – psychology, social philosophy, and ethics – enter into the study of literature' (p. 30), and discussed the great pedagogical benefits of understanding and using the reader's response. *The Reader, the Text, the Poem* (1978) elaborates and updates these ideas, emphasizing the notion of the poem as an event, and the critical centrality of this event in the author–text–reader transaction.

In 1970, Walter J. Slatoff, in a book with no particular or explicit theoretical pretensions, *With Respect to Readers: Dimensions of Literary Response*, pointed out that the discrepancy between the private experience of reading and the public activity of analysis marks an insufficiency or an evasion in our accounts of the complex relationship between form and response. The book makes a plea for some attention to reading as an activity which contaminates and complicates the autonomy of literary works and the illusory purity of a formalist approach. Slatoff urges an awareness of the discrepancy between the language of literature and the language of response to literature; between the experience of reading (which can be disruptive, disordering, discomfiting) and the emphases required by formalist literary study (the overemphasis, for instance, on unity, order, harmony). Slatoff's view is that aesthetic contemplation makes one aware of one's relation to the object and thus of the self; and that the phenomenon of difference (different selves, different thresholds of response, different sensory perceptions, etc.) as well as agreement in literary response should be granted some measure of significance.

4 For a succinct introduction to the philosophical orientations and the reading strategies that go under the name of deconstruction see Christopher Norris (1982).

5 Knapp and Michaels's essay elicited, according to the editor of

Critical Inquiry, a 'record' number of responses to some of which most of the June 1983 issue of the journal is devoted. See also Stanley Fish (1985). Unrelated to this particular debate, but of related interest, is Paul de Man's difficult essay 'The resistance to theory' (1982).

1   Richards revisited

1 For accounts of the British social and intellectual milieus in which modern Anglo-American academic criticism was established see chapter 1 of Francis Mulhern's *The Moment of 'Scrutiny'* (1979), and chapter 1 of Terry Eagleton's *Literary Theory* (1983).
2 See Berthoff (1982) for an excellent account of the later neglected Richards.
3 *How to Read a Page* (1942) is a demonstration of this thesis.

2   New Criticism and the avoidance of reading

1 It is useful and interesting at this juncture to invoke Roman Jakobson's famous model which squares the circuit of communication more precisely and elegantly than Richards's by multiplying the three basic elements into the *six* constituent factors (together with their six corresponding functions) which comprise any speech event:

context (referential)
message (poetic)
addresser (emotive) ——————— addressee (conative)
contact (phatic)
code (metalingual)

In this model, as in Richards's, meaning does not reside in any single element but derives from the total transaction of elements. At the same time, the isolation of the *message* as a discrete, self-referential element enables Jakobson neatly to formulate the poetic function of language in 'objectively' linguistic rather than 'subjectively' hermeneutic terms, without undue psychological complications arising from emotive or conative interference. (An older Richards paid generous tribute to, and also made astute criticisms of, Jakobson's work as the fulfilment of his own ambitions.) Poetic language, in the view that became the apotheosis of the American formalist–structuralist confederacy, is that which promotes the palpability of signs, a verbal structure drawing attention to itself as language, in all its self-reflexive thickness or deviance, rather than as transparent intentionality, referentiality or affect. See the discussion in chapter 3.

2 'New Criticism', Terry Eagleton declares (*Literary Theory*, 1983), 'was the [agrarian] ideology of an uprooted, defensive intelligentsia, who reinvented in literature what they could not locate in reality' (p. 47); its main contribution to literary studies was 'to convert the poem into a fetish' (p. 49). For other accounts, see Murray Krieger, *The New Apologists for Poetry* (1977, first published 1956); Paul de Man, 'Form and intent in the American New Criticism', in *Blindness and Insight* (1983, first published 1971); Gerald Graff, 'What was New Criticism?' in *Literature Against Itself* (1979).

3 I have deliberately omitted reference to Kenneth Burke's prodigious and eclectic output which defies conventional categorization; a contemporary of the New Critics, his affinities with their academic and pedagogical concerns is negligible. Vastly important in resurrecting a new interest in rhetoric, Burke's voraciously antithetical genius has never been identified with any single critical movement.

3 The inscribed reader: Jonathan Culler and structuralist poetics

1 A representative account of structuralist aims is Tzvetan Todorov's *The Poetics of Prose* (1977).

2 For an unbiased account see Terence Hawkes, *Structuralism and Semiotics* (1977). Jonathan Culler's *Structuralist Poetics* (1975) has become a classic. For different aspects of structuralism see the 1966 issue of *Yale French Studies* devoted to the subject. For a good critique of structuralism see Fredric Jameson, *The Prison-House of Language: A Critical Account of Structuralism and Russian Formalism* (1972). For a concise account of Saussure see Jonathan Culler, *Ferdinand de Saussure* (1976).

3 For an engagement with the implications of this argument see Elizabeth Freund, '*Twelfth Night* and the tyranny of interpretation', *English Literary History*, 1986, 471–89.

4 According to this theory, the reader's construal of the text takes place in two stages of reading. On an initial, 'heuristic' reading, the reader apprehends meaning in a mimetic or referential fashion, but on this level he encounters certain contradictions, deviations or distortions ('ungrammaticalities'). This set of difficulties gives rise to, and can be resolved in, a second 'retroactive' reading. 'The ungrammaticalities spotted at the mimetic level are eventually integrated into another system' so

that that which is ungrammatical in one system (e.g. the textual or referential) is perfectly grammatical in another (e.g. the intertextual or self-referential). This second reading Riffaterre calls the 'truly hermeneutic' level. The hermeneutic reading 'hurdles' mimesis, and is the one in which the semiotic process takes place – always in the mind of a reader who, however, is 'under strict guidance and control as he fills the gaps and solves the puzzles' (p. 165). Reading and making sense, on this view, impose rigid structures to delimit and arrest the free play of the signifier. Whatever our views of this theoretical foreclosure may be, what remains remarkable about Riffaterre's theory of reading is its ability to weld theory and practice in a single and pedagogically compelling performance.

See also Riffaterre, 'Interpretation and descriptive poetry: a reading of Wordsworth's "Yew Trees"' (1973), and Geoffrey Hartman's witty riposte, 'The use and abuse of structural analysis: Riffaterre's interpretation of Wordsworth's "Yew Trees"', (1975).

5 Two central directions can be discriminated: in one the reader is identified with a coded position in the text; in the other, the activities of an empirical reader are described. Representative theorists of the first position are Genette (1980) and Prince (1980a, 1980b). Prince uses Genette's concept of the narratee – a figure, narrated in the text, who is the recipient of the text – to generate a taxonomy of readers to be used as a tool of analysis, and a typology of narratives which makes it possible to classify fictions according not only to the types of narrators but also to the types of narratees. Representative theorists of the second position, according to which an empirical reader is invited by the text to perform certain operations of construction ('a text always contains within itself directions for its own consumption' says Todorov (1980, p. 77)), may be found in Perry (1979) and Todorov (1977, 1980). Eco's more dialectical account (1979) of the construction of a Model Reader, who is the product of the reading process which elaborates it, straddles both positions.

6 I borrow the term from Shlomith Rimmon-Kenan, as hard-nosed a structuralist as it has been my privilege to meet.

7 Frank Lentricchia has argued somewhat churlishly (*After the New Criticism*, 1980, pp. 103–12) that Culler compromises two basic principles of structuralist thinking: that the self is another text, an intersubjective construct formed by cultural systems over which the individual has no control; and that the text is a kind of formless space of relationality, or an empty signifying chain, whose shape is determined by structured modes of reading. Structuralism, in Culler's account, is 'converted wholesale . . . into

a literary methodology of global implication', reifying both text and self whilst fudging the question (also fudged by Northrop Frye) of whether 'structure or system is a creation of the critical enterprise' or whether it sits 'latently under the whole range of Western literary texts' (p. 107).

8 For a lively and succinct staging of this debate see the exchange between J. Hillis Miller (1980) and Shlomith Rimmon-Kenan (1980–1) in the pages of *Poetics Today*.

4   Literature in the reader: Stanley Fish and affective poetics

1 Stephen Booth's account of 'the line-to-line experience of reading Shakespeare's sonnets' in *An Essay on Shakespeare's Sonnets* (1969) appeared hard on the heels of *Surprised by Sin*. Booth argues that since 'a poem is an experience in time' (p. 118), the reader's mind is compelled to move back and forth between different frames of reference (formal or logical or phonetic structures). 'The reader has constantly to cope with the multitudinous organizations of a Shakespeare sonnet; he is engaged and active', but he is not overwhelmed because 'he always has the comfort and security of a frame of reference' (p. 187) even though the frames are not constant.

2 See Abrams 1979, pp. 575–81; Culler 1982, pp. 65–75; and de Man 1972, pp. 188–92.

3 For a deconstruction of this unstable polarity see Barbara Johnson, 'The critical difference: BartheS/BalZac', pp. 3–12 in *The Critical Difference: Essays in the Contemporary Rhetoric of Reading* (1980).

4 For an extended commentary on Fish's style as strategy see Susan R. Horton, 'The experience of Stanley Fish's prose or the critic as self-creating, self-consuming artificer' (1977).

5 See Walter Benn Michaels, 'The interpreter's self: Peirce on the Cartesian subject' (1977, reprinted in Tompkins 1980), for an excellent account of the problem of subjectivity and the traditional American pragmatist 'mistrust of the self'.

6 Scepticism, in his view, is only another interpretive convention; 'the project of radical doubt can never outrun the necessity of being situated; in order to doubt *everything*, including the ground one stands on, one must stand somewhere else, and that somewhere else will then be the ground on which one stands' (1980, p. 360).

7 It is also no accident that Fish's most recent concerns have

veered in the direction of the ultimate theoretical consequence of
his theoretical position which is now 'against theory' – see Knapp
and Michaels (1982), Fish (1985).

5   The relation of the reader to daydreaming: Norman Holland and transactive criticism

1 For a convenient overview of these theories see Elizabeth Wright
   (1984).
2 The editor of the *Standard Edition* notes that the piece was
   'originally delivered as a lecture on 6 December 1907, before an
   audience of 90, in the rooms of the Viennese publisher and
   bookseller Hugo Heller, who was himself a member of the
   Viennese Psycho-Analytical Society. A very accurate summary of
   the lecture appeared next day in the Viennese daily *Die Zeit*'
   (1953, IX, p. 142).
3 An important precursor is Simon O. Lesser (1957), who argued
   that we read to find satisfaction of repressed fantasies in symbolic
   representation. 'Literature gives us forms for our feelings' (p. 44),
   where form is a mode of defence or mastery: 'A whole battery of
   formal devices is called into play to prevent the anxiety from
   materializing' (p. 134), and the connection between the literary
   text and our lives is 'staged' in a place from which we are
   separated by a safe distance.
4 It is beyond my intentions or the scope of this survey to engage
   with the subtleties and frequent obscurities of Lacan's thinking.
   The reader who wishes to pursue these intricacies is referred to
   Jacques Derrida's reading of Lacan's reading of Poe: 'The
   purveyor of truth' (1975). Barbara Johnson's brilliant staging of a
   confrontation between the three texts – 'The frame of reference:
   Poe, Lacan, Derrida' – was first published in *Yale Fench Studies*
   (1977) and is reprinted in Geoffrey H. Hartman (ed.), *Psychoanalysis and the Question of the Text* (1978). See also Jeffrey
   Mehlman, 'Poe Pourri: Lacan's purloined letter' (1975).
5 See, for example, André Green (1978, 1980).
6 The difficulty is cogently described in Jane P. Tompkins's review
   of Bleich's book (1978), and also in William Ray's *Literary Meaning*
   (1984), pp. 87–9.

6   The peripatetic reader: Wolfgang Iser and the aesthetics of reception

1 The various theories tend to overburden and obfuscate rather

than clarify the main points at issue. I agree with Holub's observation that 'it is far from certain that all of these terms fit together in the neat system Iser desires . . . it is not always apparent how the two sets [of terms] relate – or if they do not in fact overlap'. The result is often a kind of theoretical over-kill: 'many concepts appropriated from other contexts bring with them connotations inimical to a basically phenomenological undertaking' (p. 101).

2 For a brief survey, see J. Hillis Miller, 'The Geneva School' (1966).

3 For a more thorough exposition and critique of Ingarden, see William Ray (1984), pp. 27–59, *passim*.

In conclusion: reading reading

1 In this respect reader-response criticisms join hands with other contemporary, post-structuralist trends in criticism to undermine the traditional concept of an objective and stable text, by replacing an aesthetics of production by an aesthetics of reception.

2 Hirsch (1967), p. 224; the appendix entitled 'Objective criticism' from which I quote was first published in 1960. Well before the inception of reader-response criticism, Hirsch tried to determine the limits of objectivity and subjectivity in the belief that unless there is something objective for the interpreter to contemplate there would be nothing for critics to talk about. The view he urges is that a text's correct verbal 'meaning' – a reconstruction of the author's aims and attitudes which are self-identical, unchanging and reproducible – can be objectively determined, and that the purpose of hermeneutics is to discover this meaning rather than the text's 'significance' or relevance. According to Hirsch, if we distinguish between the concept of 'meaning', which is identified with the author's intention and refers to the permanent verbal meaning, and the concept of 'significance', which refers to the variable constructions of the text's relevance in different historical contexts, we can then safely separate (and thus regulate) the respective activities of criticism and interpretation.

3 G. Douglas Atkins (1983) has coined the label 'reader-responsibility criticism' to describe the recent work of Geoffrey Hartman.

4 For an account of some of the consequences of reading beyond reader-response criticism, see Culler (1982), especially the section entitled 'Reading as a woman'. The remarkable recent output of feminist studies is eloquent testimony to the return of a reader whose voice has traditionally been silenced.

In a class by himself is Harold Bloom whose hybrid genre of writing defies categorization. In a sense that is more radical than any reader-response criticism Bloom has repeatedly urged the view that 'the true poem is the critic's mind': all reading is a necessary and creative 'misprision' or misunderstanding of a prior text, and the strongest critics are the poets who misinterpret (in order to swerve away from) their strongest precursors and thereby create an imaginative space for themselves. In arguing for the collapse of barriers between text and self Bloom goes beyond reader-response critics by demolishing the even more redoubtable barriers we place between the literary text and the critical text.

References

Abrams, M.H. (1958) *The Mirror and the Lamp: Romantic Theory and the Critical Tradition*. New York: Norton. (First published 1953.)

Abrams, M.H. (1977) 'The deconstructive angel', *Critical Inquiry*, 3, 425–38.

Abrams, M.H. (1979) 'How to do things with texts', *Partisan Review*, 46, 565–80.

Adams, Hazard (ed.) (1971) *Critical Theory Since Plato*. New York: Harcourt Brace Jovanovich. (First published 1941.)

Atkins, Douglas G. (1983) *Reading Deconstruction: Deconstructive Reading*. Lexington: Kentucky University Press.

Barthes, Roland (1974) *S/Z* (trans. Richard Miller). New York: Hill & Wang.

Barthes, Roland (1977) 'The death of the author', in Heath, Stephen (ed. and trans.), *Image Music Text*. New York: Hill & Wang.

Bateson, F.W. (1950) *English Poetry: A Critical Introduction*. London: Longman.

Benjamin, Walter (1969) *Illuminations*. New York: Schocken.

Benveniste, Emile (1971) *Problems in General Linguistics*. Miami: University of Miami Press.

Berthoff, Ann E. (1982) 'I.A. Richards and the audit of meaning', *New Literary History*, 14, 63–80.

Blackmur, R.P. (1955) *The Lion and the Honeycomb*. New York: Harcourt Brace and World.

Blackmur, R.P. (1952) *Language as Gesture: Essays in Poetry*. New York: Harcourt Brace and World. (First published 1935.)

Bleich, David (1978) *Subjective Criticism*. Baltimore: Johns Hopkins University Press.

Booth, Stephen (1969) *An Essay on Shakespeare's Sonnets*. New Haven: Yale University Press.

Booth, W.C. (1961) *The Rhetoric of Fiction*. Chicago: University of Chicago Press.

Booth, W.C. (1977) ' "Preserving the exemplar": or, how not to dig our own graves', *Critical Inquiry*, 3, 407–24.

Borges, Jorge Luis (1962) *Labyrinths* (ed. Donald A. Yates and James E. Irby). Harmondsworth: Penguin.

Brooks, Cleanth (1947) *The Well-Wrought Urn: Studies in the Structure of Poetry*. New York: Harcourt Brace and Co.

Brooks, Cleanth (1951) 'Irony as a principle of structure', in Zabel, M.D. (ed.), *Literary Opinion in America*. New York: Harper.

Brooks, Cleanth, and Warren, R.P. (1943) *Understanding Fiction*. New York: Appleton–Century–Crofts.

Brooks, Cleanth, and Warren, R.P. (1960) *Understanding Poetry*. New York: Holt, Rinehart & Winston. (First published 1938.)

Crews, Frederick (1975) *Out of My System: Psychoanalysis, Ideology and Critical Method*. New York: Oxford University Press.

Culler, Jonathan (1975) *Structuralist Poetics: Structuralism, Linguistics and the Study of Literature*. Ithaca: Cornell University Press.

Culler, Jonathan (1976) *Ferdinand de Saussure*. Harmondsworth: Penguin.

Culler, Jonathan (1980) 'Prolegomena to a theory of reading', in Suleiman, Susan R. and Crosman, Inge (eds), *The Reader in the Text: Essays on Audience and Interpretation*. Princeton, NJ: Princeton University Press.

Culler, Jonathan (1981) *The Pursuit of Signs: Semiotics, Literature, Deconstruction*. London: Routledge & Kegan Paul.

Culler, Jonathan (1982) *On Deconstruction: Theory and Criticism After Structuralism*. Ithaca: Cornell University Press.

De Man, Paul (1972) 'Literature and language: a commentary', *New Literary History*, 1, 181–92.

De Man, Paul (1979) *Allegories of Reading: Figural Language in Rousseau, Nietzsche, Rilke and Proust*. New Haven: Yale University Press.

De Man, Paul (1983) *Blindness and Insight: Essays in the Rhetoric of Contemporary Criticism*. London: Methuen. (First published 1971.)

Derrida, Jacques (1975) 'The purveyor of truth', *Yale French Studies*, 52, 31–113.

Eagleton, Terry (1983) *Literary Theory: An Introduction*. Oxford: Blackwell.

Eco, Umberto (1979) *The Role of the Reader: Explorations in the Semiotics of Texts*. Bloomington: Indiana University Press.

Eliot, T.S. (1932) *Selected Essays*. London: Faber & Faber.

Empson, William (1961) *Seven Types of Ambiguity*. Harmondsworth: Peregrine. (First published 1930.)

Felman, Shoshana (1977) 'To open the question', *Yale French Studies*, 55/6, 5–10.

Fish, Stanley E. (1967) *Surprised by Sin: The Reader in Paradise Lost*. New York: St Martin's Press.

Fish, Stanley E. (1970) 'Literature in the reader: affective stylistics', *New Literary History*, 2, 123–62.

Fish, Stanley E. (1972) *Self-Consuming Artifacts: The Experience of Seventeenth-Century Literature*. Berkeley: University of California Press.

Fish, Stanley E. (1976) 'Interpreting the *Variorum*', *Critical Inquiry*, 3, 465–85.

Fish, Stanley E. (1978) 'Normal circumstances, literal language, direct speech acts, the ordinary, the everyday, the obvious, what goes without saying, and other special cases', *Critical Inquiry*, 4, 625–44.

Fish, Stanley E. (1980) *Is There a Text in This Class? The Authority of Interpretive Communities*. Cambridge, Mass.: Harvard University Press.

Fish, Stanley E. (1981) 'Why no one's afraid of Wolfgang Iser', *Diacritics*, 11, 2–13.

Fish, Stanley E. (1985) 'Consequences', *Critical Inquiry*, 3, 433–58.

Freud, Sigmund (1953) 'Creative writers and daydreaming', in *The Standard Edition of the Complete Psychological Works*. London: The Hogarth Press and the Institute of Psychoanalysis, IX, 141–54.

Freund, Elizabeth (1986) '*Twelfth Night* and the tyranny of interpretation', *English Literary History*, 471–89.

Frye, Northrop (1957) *Anatomy of Criticism: Four Essays*. Princeton, NJ: Princeton University Press.

Genette, Gérard (1980) *Narrative Discourse: An Essay in Method* (trans. Jane E. Lewin). Ithaca: Cornell University Press.

Graff, Gerald (1979) *Literature Against Itself: Literary Ideas in Modern Society*. Chicago: University of Chicago Press.

Green, André (1978) 'The double and the absent', in Roland, Alan (ed.), *Psychoanalysis, Creativity and Literature: A French–American Inquiry*. New York: Columbia University Press, 271–92.

Green, André (1980) 'The unbinding process', *New Literary History*, xii, 11–39.

Harari, Josué V. (ed.) (1979) *Textual Strategies: Perspectives in Post-Structuralist Criticism*. Ithaca: Cornell University Press.

Hartman, Geoffrey H. (1975) 'The use and abuse of structural analysis: Riffaterre's interpretation of Wordsworth's "Yew Trees" ', *New Literary History*, 7, 165–89.

Hartman, Geoffrey H. (1976) 'Literary criticism and its discontents', *Critical Inquiry*, 3, 203–20.

Hartman, Geoffrey H. (ed.) (1978) *Psychoanalysis and the Question of the Text*. Baltimore: Johns Hopkins University Press.

Hartman, Geoffrey H. (1980) *Criticism in the Wilderness: The Study of Literature Today*. New Haven: Yale University Press.

Hartman, Geoffrey H. (1981) *Saving the Text: Literature/Derrida/Philosophy*. Baltimore: Johns Hopkins University Press.

Hawkes, Terence (1977) *Structuralism and Semiotics*. London: Methuen.

Hirsch, E.D. (1967) *Validity in Interpretation*. New Haven: Yale University Press.

Holland, Norman N. (1968) *The Dynamics of Literary Response*. New York: Oxford University Press.

Holland, Norman N. (1973) *Poems in Persons: An Introduction to the Psychoanalysis of Literature*. New York: Norton.

Holland, Norman N. (1975a) *5 Readers Reading*. New Haven: Yale University Press.

Holland, Norman N. (1975b) 'UNITY IDENTITY TEXT SELF', *Proceedings of the Modern Language Association*, 90, 813–22.

Holland, Norman N. (1976) 'Literary interpretation and three phases of psychoanalysis', *Critical Inquiry*, 3, 221–33.

Holland, Norman N. (1978) 'How can Dr Johnson's remarks on Cordelia's death add to my own response?', in Hartman, Geoffrey H. (ed.), *Psychoanalysis and the Question of the Text*. Baltimore: Johns Hopkins University Press.

Holland, Norman N. (1980a) 'Re-covering "The Purloined Letter": reading as a personal transaction', in Suleiman, Susan R. and Crosman, Inge (eds), *The Reader in the Text: Essays on Audience and Interpretation*. Princeton, NJ: Princeton University Press.

Holland, Norman N. (1980b) 'Hermia's dream', in Schwartz, Murray, and Kahn, Coppélia (eds), *Representing Shakespeare*. Baltimore: Johns Hopkins University Press.

Holland, Norman N. (1982) 'Why this is transference, nor am I out of it', *Psychoanalysis and Contemporary Thought*, 5, 27–34.

Holub, Robert C. (1984) *Reception Theory: A Critical Introduction*. London: Methuen.

Horton, Susan R. (1977) 'The experience of Stanley Fish's prose or the critic as self-creating, self-consuming artificer', *Genre*, 10, 443–53.

Hoy, David Couzens (1980) *The Critical Circle: Literature, History and Philosophical Hermeneutics*. Berkeley: University of California Press. (First published 1978.)

Ingarden, Roman (1973) *The Literary Work of Art: An Investigation on the Borderlines of Ontology, Logic and the Theory of Literature*. Evanston, Ill.:

Northwestern University Press. (First published in Polish, 1931.)

Iser, Wolfgang (1971a) 'The reading process: a phenomenological approach', *New Literary History*, 3, 279–99.

Iser, Wolfgang (1971b) 'Indeterminacy and the reader's response to prose fiction', in Miller, J. Hillis (ed.), *Aspects of Narrative*. New York: Columbia University Press.

Iser, Wolfgang (1974) *The Implied Reader: Patterns of Communication in Prose Fiction from Bunyan to Beckett*. Baltimore: Johns Hopkins University Press.

Iser, Wolfgang (1978) *The Act of Reading: A Theory of Aesthetic Response*. Baltimore: Johns Hopkins University Press.

Iser, Wolfgang (1980) 'Interaction between text and reader', in Suleiman, Susan, and Crosman, Inge (eds), *The Reader in the Text: Essays on Audience and Interpretation*. Princeton, NJ: Princeton University Press.

Iser, Wolfgang (1981) 'Talk like whales', *Diacritics*, 11, 82–7.

Jakobson, Roman (1960) 'Closing statement: linguistics and poetics', in Sebeok, T.A. (ed.), *Style in Language*. Cambridge, Mass.: MIT Press.

Jakobson, Roman, and Lévi-Strauss, Claude (1962) '*Les Chats* de Charles Baudelaire', *L'Homme*, 2, 5–21.

Jakobson, Roman, and Jones, Lawrence G. (1970) *Shakespeare's Verbal Art in 'Th'Expence of Spirit'*. The Hague: Mouton.

Jameson, Fredric (1972) *The Prison-House of Language: A Critical Account of Structuralism and Russian Formalism*. Princeton, NJ: Princeton University Press.

Jauss, Hans Robert (1982) *Toward an Aesthetic of Reception* (trans. Timothy Bahti). Minneapolis: University of Minnesota Press.

Johnson, Barbara (1977) 'The frame of reference: Poe, Lacan, Derrida', *Yale French Studies*, 55/6, 457–505.

Johnson, Barbara (1980) *The Critical Difference: Essays in the Contemporary Rhetoric of Reading*. Baltimore: Johns Hopkins University Press.

Knapp, Stephen, and Michaels, Walter Benn (1982) 'Against theory', *Critical Inquiry*, 8, 723–42.

Krieger, Murray (1976) *Theory of Criticism: A Tradition and its System*. Baltimore: Johns Hopkins University Press.

Krieger, Murray (1977) *The New Apologists for Poetry*. Westport, Conn.: Greenwood Press. (First published 1956).

Kris, Ernst (1964) *Psychoanalytic Explorations in Art*. New York: Schocken. (First published 1952.)

Lacan, Jacques (1972) 'Seminar on "The Purloined Letter"', *Yale French Studies*, 48, 38–72.

Lentricchia, Frank (1980) *After the New Criticism*. Chicago: University of Chicago Press.

Lesser, Simon O. (1957) *Fiction and the Unconscious*. Boston: Vintage.

Lotman, Yury M. (1982) 'The text and the structure of its audience', *New Literary History*, 14, 81–7.

Mailloux, Steven J. (1982) *Interpretive Conventions: The Reader in the Study of American Fiction*. Ithaca: Cornell University Press.

Mehlman, Jeffrey (1975) 'Poe Pourri: Lacan's Purloined Letter', *Semiotexte*, 1, 51–68.

Michaels, Walter Benn (1977) 'The interpreter's self: Peirce on the Cartesian subject', *Georgia Review*, 31, 383–402.

Michaels, Walter Benn (1979) 'Against formalism: the autonomous text in legal and literary interpretation', *Poetics Today*, 1, 23–34.

Miller, J. Hillis (1966) 'The Geneva School', *Critical Quarterly*, 8, 305–21.

Miller, J. Hillis (1980) 'The figure in the carpet', *Poetics Today*, 1, 3, 107–18.

Miller, J. Hillis (1980/81) 'A guest in the house. Reply to Shlomith Rimmon-Kenan's Reply', *Poetics Today*, 2, 1b, 189–91.

Mulhern, Francis (1979) *The Moment of 'Scrutiny'*. London: New Left Books.

Nelson, Cary (1976) 'Reading criticism', *Proceedings of the Modern Language Association*, 91, 801–15.

Nelson, Cary (1978) 'The psychology of criticism', in Hartman, Geoffrey H. (ed.), *Psychoanalysis and the Question of the Text*. Baltimore: Johns Hopkins University Press.

Norris, Christopher (1982) *Deconstruction: Theory and Practice*. London: Methuen.

Perry, Menakhem (1979) 'Literary dynamics: how the order of a text creates its meanings, with an analysis of Faulkner's "A Rose for Emily"', *Poetics Today*, 1, 1, 35–64 and 311–61.

Poulet, Georges (1969) 'Phenomenology of reading', *New Literary History*, 1, 53–68.

Prince, Gerald (1980a) 'Notes on the text as reader', in Suleiman, Susan R. and Crosman, Inge (eds), *The Reader in the Text: Essays on Audience and Interpretation*. Princeton, NJ: Princeton University Press.

Prince, Gerald (1980b) 'Introduction to the study of the narratee', in Tompkins, Jane (ed.), *Reader–Response Criticism*. Baltimore: Johns Hopkins University Press, 7–25.

Ransom, J.C. (1938) *The World's Body*. New York: Scribner.

Ransom, J.C. (1941) *The New Criticism*. Norfolk, Conn.: New Directions.

Ransom, J.C. (1971) 'Criticism as pure speculation', in Adams,

Hazard (ed.), *Critical Theory Since Plato*. New York: Harcourt Brace Jovanovich. (First published 1941.)

Ray, William (1984) *Literary Meaning: From Phenomenology to Deconstruction*. Oxford: Blackwell.

Richards, I.A. (1924) *Principles of Literary Criticism*. London: Routledge & Kegan Paul.

Richards, I.A. (1929) *Practical Criticism*. New York: Harcourt Brace and Co.

Richards, I.A. (1934) *Coleridge on Imagination*. London: Routledge & Kegan Paul.

Richards, I.A. (1936) *The Philosophy of Rhetoric*. Oxford: Oxford University Press.

Richards, I.A. (1942) *How to Read a Page*. New York: Norton.

Richards, I.A. (1955) *Speculative Instruments*. London: Routledge & Kegan Paul.

Richards, I.A. (1970) *Poetries and Sciences*. New York: Norton. (First published as *Science and Poetry*, 1926.)

Ricoeur, Paul (1970) *Freud and Philosophy: An Essay on Interpretation*. New Haven: Yale University Press.

Riffaterre, Michael (1966) 'Describing poetic structures: two approaches to Baudelaire's "Les Chats"', *Yale French Studies*, 36/7, 200–42.

Riffaterre, Michael (1973) 'Interpretation and descriptive poetry: a reading of Wordsworth's "Yew Trees"', *New Literary History*, 4, 229–56.

Riffaterre, Michael (1978) *The Semiotics of Poetry*. Bloomington: Indiana University Press.

Rimmon-Kenan, Shlomith (1977) *The Concept of Ambiguity – The Example of James*. Chicago: University of Chicago Press.

Rimmon-Kenan, Shlomith (1980/1) 'Deconstructive reflections on deconstruction. In reply to J. Hillis Miller', *Poetics Today*, 2, 1b, 185–8.

Rosenblatt, Louise (1937) *Literature as Exploration*. New York: Appleton–Century–Crofts.

Rosenblatt, Louise (1978) *The Reader, The Text, The Poem: The Transactional Theory of the Literary Work*. Carbondale: Southern Illinois University Press.

Slatoff, Walter J. (1970) *With Respect to Readers: Dimensions of Literary Response*. Ithaca: Cornell University Press.

Suleiman, Susan R. and Crosman, Inge, (eds) (1980) *The Reader in the Text: Essays on Audience and Interpretation*. Princeton, NJ: Princeton University Press.

Tate, Allen (1968) 'Literature as knowledge', in *Essays of Four Decades*. Chicago: Swallow Press.

Todorov, Tzvetan (1977) *The Poetics of Prose*. Ithaca: Cornell University Press. (First published in French, 1971.)

Todorov, Tzvetan (1980) 'Reading as construction', in Suleiman, Susan and Crosman, Inge (eds), *The Reader in the Text: Essays on Audience and Interpretation*. Princeton, NJ: Princeton University Press.

Tompkins, Jane P. (1978) 'Review of David Bleich's *Subjective Criticism*', *Modern Language Notes*, 93, 1068–75.

Tompkins, Jane P. (1980) *Reader–Response Criticism: From Formalism to Post-Structuralism*. Baltimore: Johns Hopkins University Press.

Trilling, Lionel (1961) 'Freud and literature', in *The Liberal Imagination*. London: Mercury. (First published 1951.)

Warren, R.P. (1958) 'Pure and impure poetry', in *Selected Essays*. New York: Random House.

Wellek, René, and Warren, Austin (1949) *Theory of Literature*. London: Cape. (First published 1949.)

Wimsatt, W.K. (1970a) *The Verbal Icon: Studies in the Meaning of Poetry*. London: Methuen. (First published 1954.)

Wimsatt, W.K. (1970b) 'Battering the object: the ontological approach', in Bradbury, Malcolm, and Palmer, David (eds), *Contemporary Criticism*. London: Edward Arnold.

Wright, Elisabeth (1984) *Psychoanalytic Criticism: Theory and Practice*. London: Methuen.

Further reading

Altick, Richard (1932) *The English Common Reader: A Social History of the Mass Reading Public, 1800–1900*. London: Chatto & Windus.

Austin, J.L. (1975) *How To Do Things With Words*. Cambridge, Mass.: Harvard University Press.

Barthes, Roland (1975) *The Pleasure of the Text* (trans. Richard Miller). New York: Hill & Wang.

Beardsley, C. Monroe (1958) *Aesthetics: Problems in the Philosophy of Criticism*. New York: Harcourt Brace and World.

Black, Stephen A. (1977) 'On reading psychoanalytically', *College English*, 39, 267–75.

Bleich, David (1975) *Readings and Feelings: An Introduction to Subjective Criticism*. Urbana, Ill.: National Council of Teachers of English.

Bloom, Harold (1973) *The Anxiety of Influence: A Theory of Poetry*. New York: Oxford University Press.

Bloom, Harold (1975) *Kabbalah and Criticism*. New York: Seabury Press.

Bloom, Harold (1975) *A Map of Misreading*. New York: Oxford University Press.

Bloom, Harold (1982) *Agon: Towards a Theory of Revisionism*. New York: Oxford University Press.

Bloom, Harold, de Man, Paul, Derrida, Jacques, Hartman, Geoffrey, and Miller, J. Hillis (1979) *Deconstruction and Criticism*. New York: Seabury Press.

Booth, Stephen (1969) 'On the value of *Hamlet*', in Rabkin, Norman, (ed.), *Reinterpretation of Elizabethan Drama*. New York: Columbia University Press.

Booth, Wayne (1979) *Critical Understanding: The Powers and Limits of Pluralism*. Chicago: University of Chicago Press.

Brooke-Rose, Christine (1980) 'The readerhood of man', in Suleiman, Susan R., and Crosman, Inge, (eds), *The Reader in the Text: Essays on Audience and Interpretation*. Princeton, NJ: Princeton University Press, 120–48.

Brooke-Rose, Christine (1980) 'Round and round the Jakobson diagram: a survey', *Hebrew University Studies in Literature*, 8, 153–82.

Brooks, Peter (1976) 'Competent readers', *Diacritics*, 6, 23–6.

Brower, Reuben, Vendler, Helen, and Hollander, John (eds) (1973) *I.A. Richards: Essays in His Honour*. New York: Oxford University Press.

Burns, Elizabeth, and Burns, Tom, (eds) (1973) *Sociology of Literature and Drama*. Harmondsworth: Penguin.

Charles, Michel (1977) *Rhetorique de la Lecture*. Paris: Seuil.

Crews, Frederick (ed.) (1970) *Psychoanalysis and Literary Process*. Berkeley: University of California Press.

Crosman, Robert (1980) 'Do readers make meaning?', in Suleiman, Susan R., and Crosman, Inge (eds), *The Reader in the Text: Essays on Audience and Interpretation*. Princeton, NJ: Princeton University Press.

Crosman, Inge (1980) 'Bibliography of audience-oriented criticism', in Suleiman, Susan R. and Crosman, Inge (eds), *The Reader in the Text: Essays on Audience and Interpretation*. Princeton, NJ: Princeton University Press.

De Man, Paul (1969) 'The rhetoric of temporality', in Singleton, Charles S. (ed.), *Interpretation: Theory and Practice*. Baltimore: Johns Hopkins University Press.

De Man, Paul (1982) 'The resistance to literary theory', *Yale French Studies*, 63, 3–20.

De Maria, Robert, Jr (1978) 'The ideal reader: a critical fiction', *Proceedings of the Modern Language Association*, 93, 463–74.

Derrida, Jacques (1976) *Of Grammatology* (trans. Gayatri Chakravorty Spivak). Baltimore: Johns Hopkins University Press.

Dillon, George (1978) *Language Processing and the Reading of Literature: Towards a Model of Comprehension*. Bloomington: Indiana University Press.

Erlich, Victor (1975) 'Reading conscious and unconscious', *College English*, 36, 766–75.

Fekete, John (1977) *The Critical Twilight*. London: Routledge & Kegan Paul.

Felman, Shoshana (1977) 'Turning the screw of interpretation', *Yale French Studies*, 55/6, 94–207.

176   Further reading

Fetterly, Judith (1979) *The Resisting Reader: A Feminist Approach to American Fiction*. Bloomington: Indiana University Press.

Fokkema, Douwe Wessel, and Elrud, Kunne-Ibsch (1978) *Theories of Literature in the Twentieth Century: Structuralism, Marxism, Aesthetics of Reception*. New York: St Martin's Press.

Garwin, Harry R. (ed.) (1981) *Theories of Reading, Looking and Listening* (reissue of *Bucknell Review*, 28). London: Associated University Press.

Gibson, Walker (1950) 'Authors, speakers, readers, mock readers', *College English*, 11, 265–9.

Gombrich, E.H. (1962) *Art and Illusion: A Study in the Psychology of Pictorial Representation*. London: Phaidon Press.

Harding, D.W. (1937) 'The role of the onlooker', *Scrutiny*, 6, 247–58.

Harding, D.W. (1962) 'Psychological processes in the reading of fiction', *British Journal of Aesthetics*, 2, 133–47.

Hartman, Geoffrey H. (1970) *Beyond Formalism: Literary Essays 1958–1970*. New Haven: Yale University Press.

Hartman, Geoffrey H. (1975) *The Fate of Reading*. Chicago: University of Chicago Press.

Hartman, Geoffrey H. (1983) 'The new wilderness: critics as connoisseurs of chaos', in Hassan, Ihab, and Hassan, Sally (eds) *Innovation/Renovation: New Perspectives on the Humanities*. Madison: University of Wisconsin Press.

Hartman, Geoffrey H. (1984) 'The culture of criticism', *Proceedings of the Modern Language Association*, 99, 371–97.

Holland, Norman N. (1982) *Laughing: A Psychology of Humour*. Ithaca: Cornell University Press.

Holland, Norman N. (1985) *The I*. New Haven: Yale University Press.

Kincaid, James R. (1977) 'Coherent readers, incoherent texts', *Critical Inquiry*, 3, 701–802.

Kintgen, Eugene R. (1977) 'Reader response and stylistics', *Style*, 11, 1–18.

Leavis, Q.D. (1932) *Fiction and the Reading Public*. London: Chatto & Windus.

Leitch, Vincent B. (1983) *Deconstructive Criticism: An Advanced Introduction*. London: Hutchinson.

Melnick, Daniel (1979) 'Fullness and dissonance: music and the reader's experience of modern fiction', *Modern Fiction Studies*, 25, 209–22.

Ong, Walter J., SJ (1975) 'The writer's audience is always a fiction', *Proceedings of the Modern Language Association*, 90, 9–21.

Purves, Alan C. (ed.) (1972) *How Porcupines Make Love: Notes on a*

Response-Centered Curriculum. Lexington, Mass.: Xerox Publishing Co.

Purves, Alan C., and Beach, Richard (1972) *Literature and the Reader: Research in Response to Literature, Reading Interests, and the Teaching of Literature.* Urbana, Ill.: National Council of Teachers of English.

Rabinowitz, Peter (1977) 'Truth in fiction: a re-examination of audiences', *Critical Inquiry,* 4, 121–41.

Rabinowitz, Peter (1980) ' "What's Hecuba to us?" The audience's experience of literary borrowing', in Suleiman, Susan R., and Crosman, Inge (eds), *The Reader in the Text: Essays on Audience and Interpretation.* Princeton, NJ: Princeton University Press.

Schwartz, Murray (1975) 'Where is literature?', *College English,* 36, 756–65.

Smith, Joseph H., (ed.) (1980) *The Literary Freud: Mechanisms of Defence and the Poetic Will.* New Haven: Yale University Press.

Steiner, George (1979) ' "Critic"/"Reader" ', *New Literary History,* 10, 423–52.

Tompkins, Jane (1977) 'Criticism and feeling', *College English,* 39, 169–78.

Tompkins, Jane (ed.) (1980) 'Bibliography', in *Reader-Response Criticism.* Baltimore: Johns Hopkins University Press, 233–71.

Wellek, René (1978) 'The New Criticism: pro and contra', *Critical Inquiry,* 4, 611–24.

Young, Robert (1981) *Untying the Text: A Post-Structuralist Reader.* London: Routledge & Kegan Paul.

Index

codes: interpretive 107–8;
    linguistic 12, 74, 76, 78
cognitive value of poetry 28, 50;
    emphasized by New Critics 41;
    repressed by Richards's
    students 32
Coleridgean theory of mind 27,
    57, 59
colloquial speech 74
communication: endangered by
    ambiguity 47–9; endangered
    by stock responses 33–5, 43;
    foregrounding of the message
    in 74–5, 78, 107; as a 'two-way
    relationship' 143; see also
    hermeneutics
'competence': and
    conventionality 82, 106; in
    Culler 80–5; and Fish 96, 110;
    see also informed reader
content, 'unconscious' 122
contradiction, in Empson 47–9
convention, and interpretation,
    see interpretation
Crews, Frederick 122
criticism, Anglo-American 1,
    3–7, 9–13, 105, 148; adaptation
    of structuralism by 69; crisis in
    19, 63, 65; importance of New
    Critics in 51, 64; importance of
    Richards in 23, 36; and psycho-
    analysis 113
Culler, Jonathan: critique of
    Holland 127; and
    deconstruction 70, 85–9, 153,
    157n.2; On Deconstruction 85;
    and the ideal reader 7, 82–3,
    84; on institutional aspects of
    response 36, 80–5, 130; view of
    New Criticism 63–4;
    Structuralist Poetics 70; and
    structuralist theories of
    reading 70–2, 75, 78–89, 136,
    161n.7

daydreaming, see fantasy
deconstruction 18; and Derrida
    11; and reading 70, 85–9, 155
de Man, Paul 18, 51, 57, 89, 94,
    154, 156; critique of Empson
    46–7
Derrida, Jacques 11, 103, 126
diachronicity 59; see also history
'dialectical' text, as against
    'rhetorical' 97–104, 107
'difference', as place of meaning
    19, 38, 82
displacement 115–16, 126
Donne, John 52, 97

Eagleton, Terry: Literary Theory
    159n.1, 160n.2
Eco, Umberto 7
ego: and interpretation 128; and
    phenomenology 138–9;
    relation to id 118; unity of 121,
    123, 126; and writing 115–17
ego-psychology, American 113
Eliot, T. S. 40; 'The Function of
    Criticism' 4; and
    impersonality 4, 5, 34
Empson, William 41; and
    ambiguity 43–9; and irony 54;
    Seven Types of Ambiguity 44, 119
'event', text as 93–5; see also text
experience, see event; reader

'fact', and interpretation 83, 88,
    94, 104, 151–2
fantasy, art's relation to 115–18,
    120, 124
Faulkner, William 124
Felman, Shoshana 113, 133
feminist studies, and reader-
    response criticism 164n.4
Fish, Stanley 9, 10, 83, 162n.4;
    and authority of the reader 7,
    92–6, 100–4, 106, 110, 153;
    debate with Iser 148–51;

184 Index